A Cry of Absence

OTHER BOOKS BY MARTIN E. MARTY

A Short History of Christianity

The New Shape of American Religion

The Improper Opinion

The Infidel

Baptism

The Hidden Discipline

Second Chance for American Protestants

Church Unity and Church Mission

Varieties of Unbelief

The Search for a Usable Future

The Modern Schism

Righteous Empire

Protestantism

You Are Promise

The Fire We Can Light

The Pro and Con Book of Religious America

A Nation of Behavers

Religion, Awakening and Revolution

The Lord's Supper

Friendship

By Way of Response

The Public Church

Being Good and Doing Good

Christian Churches in the United States

Christianity in the New World

Pilgrims in Their Own Land

Modern American Religion: Volume 1, The Irony of It All

Modern American Religion: Volume 2, The Noise of Conflict

Protestantism in the United States

Religion and Republic

Fundamentalisms Observed: Volume 1

The Glory and the Power: The Fundamentalist Challenge
to the Modern World

Martin E. Marty

A Cry of Absence

Reflections for the Winter of the Heart

Illustrated by
Susan Teumer Marty

HarperSanFrancisco
A Division of HarperCollinsPublishers

The text of the psalms is from the New English Bible, © The Delegates of the Oxford University Press and the Syndics of the Cambridge University Press 1961, 1970. Reprinted by permission.

I also wish to thank the following publishers for permitting quotations from their works: Alfred A. Knopf for four lines of "Winter Remembered" from John Crowe Ransom, *Selected Poems* (1963), copyright 1924, 1927, 1934, 1939, 1945, © 1962, 1963 by Alfred A. Knopf, Inc.; Oxford University Press for a quotation from Friedrich Heiler, *Prayer* (1958), pp. 283–84, copyright 1932 by Oxford University Press; The University of Chicago Press for a citation from Frederick A. Olafson, *The Dialectic of Action: A Philosophical Interpretation of History and the Humanities* (1979), pp. 255–56, © 1979 by The University of Chicago; New Directions Publishing Corporation for three short quotations from Lars Gustafsson, *The Death of a Beekeeper* (1981), pp. 78–79, copyright 1978 by Lars Gustafsson.

Library of Congress Cataloging-in-Publication Data

Marty, Martin E.
    A cry of absence: reflections for the winter of the heart /
Martin E. Marty.
      p.   cm.
    Originally published: San Francisco: Harper & Row, c1983.
    ISBN 0–06–065402–3
    1. Consolation. 2. Spiritual life—Christianity. I. Title.
[BV4905.2.M29 1993]
248.8'6—dc20   92–53217
                                                                CIP

93 94 95 96 97 CWI 10 9 8 7 6 5 4 3 2 1

To
Wesley Carlson
Susan Teumer Marty
Connie Jaarsma Marty
"in-law"
with affection

Contents

Acknowledgments

I thank Delores Smith, Assistant to the Dean of the Divinity School of the University of Chicago, for making possible the preparation of the manuscript. And my gratitude goes once again to members of the Divinity School staff who deciphered my handwritten editing and amateur typing and through successive drafts prepared the manuscript: Rehova Arthur, Martha Morrow, and Nathelda McGee. R. Scott Appleby was helpful with editing.

Preface

SHE: What happened to Psalm 88? Why did you skip it?

HE: I didn't think you could take it tonight. I am not sure I could. No: I am *sure* I could not.

SHE: Please read it, for me.

HE: All right:

> *. . . I cry out in the night before thee . . .*
> *For my soul is full of troubles . . .*
> *Thou hast put me in the depths of the Pit,*
>   *in the regions dark and deep . . .*

SHE: I need that kind the most.

In that midnight exchange, though its author did not yet know it, this book, *A Cry of Absence*, was beginning to be conceived. (See pp. 88ff.)

In the little exchange above, "she" was Elsa, whom I married forty years before this second edition of a book occasioned by her illness (pp 161–62) and after her death (p. 39), and who died a dozen years ago. I had agreed, through the seasons of her terminal illness, to take turns with her reading a biblical psalm at the time of each midnight taking of medication. The medicines were pain relievers, fighters against nausea, palliatives. Half the psalms were not.

I had agreed to read the even-numbered and she the odd-numbered psalms. But after a particularly wretched day's bout that wracked her body and my soul, I did not feel up to reading Psalm 88. She noticed that. After the conversation I have recorded here, we continued to speak, slowly and quietly, in the bleakness of midnight but in the warmth of each other's presence and in awareness of the Presence.

We agreed that often the starkest scriptures were the most credible signals of the Presence and came in the worst times. When life gets down to basics, of course one wants the consoling words, the comforting sayings, the voices of hope preserved on printed pages. But they make sense only against the background of, and in interplay with, the dark words. Dark/light. Night/day. Winter/summer: yes, here was a "wintry sort of spirituality." That phrase about winter by the Catholic theologian Karl Rahner came to mind and later got wedded to our midnight experiences.

After Elsa's death a kind dean urged me to take a winter quarter off from teaching. I would rise at four in the morning, let the snow blow past the study window, and hear the sound, not of the classical music that usually accompanies my writing, but of the wind. Only the wind. One of my ways of "working through the experience" was to write. A farseeing new acquaintance spelled these cold and dark times with the gift of flights to "summery" California and hospitality there. The trips were ostensibly for a scriptwriting assignment, but retrospect tells me he acted out of therapeutic regard for me during the development of what turned out to be a profound friendship. (One line of Psalm 88 never came true for Elsa and me: "Thou hast caused lover and friend to shun me. . . .")

In this preface I have deliberately given the page numbers of three specific passages of the book. My rereading suggests that they are the *only* three direct autobiographical allusions in this work. For the new edition I was asked to draw back the curtains from some of the midnight, midwinter experiences and "set the stage" for the book. This I am doing on these pages.

Why the diffidence the first time, and my not-all-that-revealing approach this second time? My late wife was a very private person who never bargained on having her intimate life details told to the public just because she married a garrulous and prolific speaker and writer. The two or three times during her illness that I wrote about her in my weekly column, I showed her the manuscript and got her permission before publishing. She cannot give her permission now, which is why I am not saying much more now.

There were other reasons as well. I had read searing autobiographical works like C. S. Lewis's *A Grief Observed*, and felt no calling to replicate the genre or compete for attention with the many books of that sort, moved as I was by Lewis and others. Then, too, I am an academic, and we are trained not to put too much of ourselves into our books.

The editor of the weekly column I write insisted from day one that "the word *I* should appear in it every week." But comparing notes with other columnists, I have come to know that we columnists invent a kind of replica of ourselves who sits a few inches away during the writing, an invention that prevents us from splattering psyche or, as they say, in a vulgarization of biblical terminology, "spilling our guts" every week. The columnist's "I" is "not-I," in strange ways. The genre of *A Cry of Absence* allows for more of the real I than does such an invention, but in indirect ways.

Finally, however, I had a better motive than all but the first of these for choosing not to detail the story of an illness and death. The goal, mission, dream—call it what you will—for this book was to be as helpful as possible to people in their various pilgrimages without distracting them by telling someone else's story. I knew that at our house during the bad days we had a hard time finding books that did not say "Cheer up!" or "All will be sunny, because God loves you, and so do the authors!" Books of despair, unmarked by the hope that I hope shines through by the end of this one, or books of easy solace, which is no solace on nights that call for the realism of Psalm 88, were the most recommended but always unwelcome suggestions to us.

The response to this book through the years has been revealing. I have published over forty books, and most of them have been reviewed perhaps more frequently than they deserved; the files pile high and the archives bulge. But reviewed books by historians do not often elicit letters. *A Cry of Absence* evoked more letters than the other dozens did together.

Many of the letters came from people who knew me and knew the story of illness and death behind the book. Just as many did not, since they had the book recommended to them by friends and had no reason to know the name of a University of Chicago religious historian. Those who knew said, and even those who did not know sensed, that a death shadowed these pages. When they were reading it as an accompaniment and companion in their passage involving a death, they were empathic as they elaborated their responses.

More often, to my surprise, the absence of which they wrote (and write, still) was occasioned not by death, but by other experiences. Almost always they could be summarized under two words: "separation" or "alienation."

Thus, let me paraphrase scores of them: "Dear author: I can sense that your absence was caused by a death. I extend sympathy. I, too, have known death up close. It is terrible. All the psychological surveys say that no traumas match the loss of a spouse or a child to death. I know, I know. Don't let it take anything away from their findings or your experience as I say the following, however: but I have to say that in its own way, separation is worse. During a terminal illness, you at least get to say everything, to show and express love, and love is stronger than death."

"Let me tell you," such letters would go on, "separation is really worse. I try to piece life together and go on working and planning—while my ex-husband is six blocks down the street, entangled in the limbs of a pretty young thing for whom he shed me. His plot line continues, and I am absent from it." Or: "I have custody of the children, while she has moved on, following a path of career development, and the path to not a few bedrooms along the way." Or: "After nineteen years of loving our daughter, we find that she was born to be angry, and she is absent. We last heard she was in trouble, and we do not know where she is now—except separated from us."

Yes, I had to say as I read such letters—without being able to answer each in detail—yes, absence because of separation, absence because of alienation, can be as devastating, in their own ways, as absence because of death.

Rereading *A Cry of Absence*, which I do not feel moved to change basically after almost a dozen years, and in the tenth year of a marriage which more often than not brings its own kind of spring and sun, I found one note that might have been more developed. I refer to two sections, "The Need for Community" (p. 144) and "Congregating in the Sacred Courts" (p. 163). I grow more convinced than before that, whether in the valleys of the shadow of separation, alienation, or death, we do well to draw upon company and communion formed before, during, and after the profound experiences of life.

Writings, letters, and books can also be companions. One of the compensations of these years has been the thought that *A Cry of Absence* has been taken along the walks of those who seek the Presence. I hope in a new edition it will have thousands of new chances to do so.

1. Winter Journey: The Absence

Winter is a season of the heart as much as it is a season in the weather. John Crowe Ransom connected the two kinds of winter:

> Two evils, monstrous either one apart,
> Possessed me, and were long and loath at going;
> A cry of Absence, Absence, in the heart,
> And in the wood the furious winter blowing.

I invite the reader to undertake a journey of the soul. It will occur in the face of the threat of Absence. Some psalms will be a guide. Winter will serve as an image for the seasons of the heart.

Winterless climates there may be, but winterless souls are

hard to picture. A person can count on winter in January in intemperate northern climates, or in July in their southern counterparts. Near the equator, winter is unfelt. As for the heart, however, where can one escape the chill? When death comes, when absence creates pain—then anyone can antici-pate the season of cold. Winter can also blow into surprising regions of the heart when it is least expected. Such frigid assaults can overtake the spirit with the persistence of an ice age, the chronic cutting of an Arctic wind.

"Absence, Absence": a poet hears the cry. Winterly frost comes in the void left when love dies or a lover grows distant. Let a new love come into life or let the enduring one come close again, and summer can return to the heart. So it is in human affairs. The absence can also come, however, to a waste space left when the divine is distant, the sacred is remote, when God is silent. The wind of furious winter for a while blows without, and then grows silent as spring comes. The fury and the bleakness within the soul can re-main, no matter what the season or the weather.

Who tends the spirit where winter takes over? The Chris-tian faith and the family are prescribed to provide refuge and warmth, and for many they do. In our generations, however, to mention spirituality is to evoke images only of the long-day suns of summers. Those who begin with a sense of the void, the Absence, who live with dullness of soul, feel left out when others speak only of such bright spirituality.

Picture someone hungry for a warming of the spirit. He calls a friend who is advertised as spirit-filled. "Praise the Lord!" she responds, as she picks up the telephone. The two meet in person. One is chilly but open to stirrings, the other well characterized as full of stir. What transfer of spirit can occur when the filled person is compulsive about the sum-mer and sunshine in her heart? Never does a frown cloud her

2

face. Lips, once drawn tight in disapproval, are now drawn tight in a cosmetic smile. "The Lord wills it." Never does the storm of a troubled heart receive its chance to be heard. The Lord has satisfied every need, one hears, so it would be a sin to stare once more at the void within. Christ is the answer, the spirit is warm and no chill is ever allowed between the boards or around the windows of the soul.

After such an encounter, questions come to mind. Is the summer-style believer being honest? Will she not have to face that void some day? Is the cry of Absence, Absence, unvoiced and unheard? Or does she ignore it? Worst of all, does she have a motive to suppress it, screen it out of her stopped ears? Does the spirit make its way only in a heart that has become a windowless hall of mirrors? Must a person, to survive, choose to create a mental sound chamber that screens out the signals of the world?

Spirit: to some the word suggests only the inner world. Nowhere, in such a case, can it connect with the images one carries of the swollen bellies of the starving or of swollen streams. Must one, can one, forget the parched tongues of children or the flooding rivers of catastrophe? "I am enjoying my spiritual high," the friend seems to be saying, "and you can have one, too—so long as you create illusion. You must vacate your heart's residence near the world of reality. Relocate yourself in a hermitage of the soul." The price for such a move seems too high: If this alone be of the spirit, one thinks, it is better to live only with the mundane. In that sphere, at least, there is honesty. There, at least, one can tend to the persistent cry of the heart, the Absence that will force itself to be heard and felt.

Beyond that individual friend with her summery smile, there is also a community that is the family of the faithful. This is the congregation of believers, the church of the practicers. The cry of Absence, Absence, in the heart is supposed

3

to be heard communally. People intend to overcome the absence by becoming a gathering of the Spirit. In that circle, certainly people can be honest about the furious winter blowing in the wood of the heart! So thinks the seeker.

Just as a person can be engulfed and alone in a crowd, so can a congregation or a fellowship overlook or scorn a member. In some tribes, it is said, the magical leader performs a rite in which an errant person is "boned." The participants gather while the shaman ritually points a magic bone at the one whom the spirits are supposed to shun. Those who have observed such ceremonies report that in many cases the boned person writhes, goes into a fit and fury, and then, spent, is taken off to a hut. Weeks pass, and the person dies.

Did the bone itself do the killing? No, says the scientific observer. As an object, it was made up of the same kinds of molecules as any other bone. The act of ritual waving is what led to death. Without their having been aware of it, the people of the tribe with their eyes first followed the motion of the bone. Then they accused the victim, instinctively thereupon withdrawing their presence. The absence did the killing. The boning rite occurs in tropical cultures under the heat of the noonday summer sun. Yet figuratively the shaman and the circle of people together inflicted winter on the hapless one. With that winter, they induced dying, death.

In just such a way the summery circles of Christian believers can "bone" their victims. Some of the accused they regard as being errant, too sinful to belong in the company of sinners. Others they see as simply marginal. They have not been invited to find the center of community, or they have never been able to find it. The shaman, the magical leader or the company of leaders, sees to it that the victim gets pushed beyond the margins, back into the wintry night. Third, it may be that those who pursue the Spirit in unconventional ways, or who receive the Spirit's gift in ways that

depart from those the group cherishes, receive no support.
They are left to their own devices, and after frustration,
choose to be alone again. Honesty is their premium, aloneness their price, absence their destiny.

A SUMMERY SPIRITUALITY

What is conventional for seekers of the Spirit? Here the
evidence is clear. A person can best display the fulfilled soul
by jumping up and down. The songs of faith, say the in-
structions, have to shout the language of abundance and life.
The rites with which one passes through the stages of life
have to represent emotionally violent turns from the old self
to the born-again new being. Never look back—or within—
is the counsel. The ways of the Lord are no longer mysterious. People reduce them through easy explanations. They
burst with shadowless joy into the heart. Enjoy these ways.

Before long, in the face of such counsel, it dawns on the
seeker of shelter: the kind of warmth that the company
cherishes is not of the sort I need. Such climate does not
shelter. It screens out those who are not in the huddle. There
is more to the dawning. Maybe, one thinks, the summery
kind of spirituality has less to do with the Spirit than with
personality types, social classes, income groups, and patterns of etiquette. Not every believer can move easily into
the rhythms of country-and-western Christianity with its
foot-stomping, exuberant styles. Those styles may come
naturally and be authentic to people in some regions and
ranks. Must they be the same for everyone? The suspend-
ered, buttoned-down believer—is he ruled out of the kingdom of warmth because his personality type is restrained,
decorous, cool? The executive woman in her tailored suit
who celebrates, at least wanly, the liturgies of the church
year and rests in the quiet glow of candles on the altar—is

she only "half-saved" because she has never been smitten or slain in the Spirit, has never swooned during prostrations or possession in moments of joy? They all feel left out in the circle of the exuberant ones, and they *are* left out. For them, the cry of Absence, Absence, is more haunting after the search than before. Sometimes, in the worst cases, it turns quiet and a stillness of spirit takes its place.

The sunny friend and the summery gathering are of little help to many seekers. If such are still to have sufficient hope to inspire an address to the absence, a quieting of the furious wintry wind, where do they turn?

In the Christian remembrance and with its family, there is a third zone: that of the movement, the spiritual enterprise. In the late years of the second millennium after Christ, the winds of the spirit are said to blow—or, to be charitable, they *do* blow—in forces called charismatic or pentecostal. These are reinforced over the radio and in television images. Many best-selling Christian books having to do with nurture of the spirit are of this exultant sort.

The message in this world of spiritual best-sellers and large audiences is consistent: "Follow me, follow my prescription, think the right thoughts, and all the chill will disappear. Joy comes to those who prosper in faith." Christ is said to be the answer, no matter what the question, no matter whether it has been carefully asked. God is immediately present; "I know, I have talked with him," says the evangelizer or the peddler. Send ten dollars, turn the dial to our program, buy the book—whatever the form of the counsel, it always amounts to the same thing—and the abundant life of sunshine and joy will be yours.

Many serious people who seek are repelled by such appeals. They turn off the television station before its thousandth repetition turns their desires into Siberias of the heart. They do not belong, they feel, to the region where sunshine language comes so easily. Their social class is too low, or too high, for its cultivated enthusiasms. Where they come from, geographically and psychologically, the calculated "looseness" of Pentecostal styles does not come naturally. They see no motive for regarding its expression supernaturally, as if the Spirit can find no other channels. They remain out in the chill, by choice, excluded or self-excluded by the charismatic style. Must conversion represent a personality change to a style that they do not find attractive, one that they do feel would be inauthentic?

Not all who stand apart do so out of snobbishness. They sometimes for a while continue their walk in the wintry woods and cast occasional longing eyes on the cabins through whose windows the glow of warmth and familiality shines. They smell the smoke from the wood fire beneath the chimneys of such spiritual lodges and envy those who find them congenial. Still, such seekers must move on in search of proper hostels. In recent years, the more staid and reserved believers have grown more tolerant of the enthusiastic, summery sorts. The patient ones come to have an aesthetic appreciation of a sort they never expected to develop. They can create enough empathy for such soulful expression that they, too, can hear and maybe even sing "Amazing Grace," where their ears and tongues had once been ready only for Gregorian chant or Lutheran chorales. They learn momentarily to identify, but they cannot remain in, the abodes of the exuberant.

Let there be, then, the responsive believer pleads, no war between spiritual styles, but only a peaceful coexistence. Rather than have one version force the other out, can they not complement each other? Each can appeal to a company of people making its pilgrimage. Each style, for that mat-

7

ter, can bring some gifts to people of the other style. There will almost inevitably be moments in the life of the summery sorts when the wintry style will speak with clarity and bracing purpose. There will also be moments in the life of the wintry sorts when the sunny style will bathe corners of their hearts with unanticipated but welcomed warmth. No logical, psychological, biblical, or traditional reasons exist to force the two to exclude each other. But there are reasons on all of those grounds for the believing community and personal seekers today to discover or to rediscover the wintry sort. It merits notice and nurture after an epoch of neglect.

To call for two styles and to find impetus for the wintry sort of search demands boldness. It receives so little attention that anyone who defends it may well express the old reformers' anxiety: am I alone right, and is the whole church wrong? Why in our era does the Christian public relations industry speak only of one style? Is the wintry kind to be forgotten, after its honored place for centuries? Has something happened in human evolution to screen out the factors that once saw the spirituality of the wintry heart to be so natural, so common? Worse, have market conditions led the advertisers to concentrate on what in slang is known as the "quick fix" in matters of the spirit?

While seeking boldness and strength in the wind and the storm, a person relies on landmarks. In a blizzard, a "whiteout" can disorient, until a wanderer cannot know whether a dark object is a match cover nearby in the snow or a hut farther away on the horizon. The seeker reaches for known, locatable objects. There must be a place to lean, to hold on. Those trained in scholarly traditions reach for authorities, for people who can prop up their pages, because the footnotes of these notable thinkers are heavy, their reputations carry weight, and their words give sureness to their step.

Karl rahner and "the wintry sort"

For this winterward part of the pilgrimage, the authority is Karl Rahner. For a third of a century the great German thinker emitted signals to guide more than the members of the Catholic church out of which he spoke. A difficult, somewhat remote figure, he was unable to use the English language, and this limited the popularity he well deserved. Rahner instead generated a kind of trickle-down influence through seminaries and seminarians. Lay people who never knew that he helped push back the encroachments of the night and the chill still profit from what he taught their leaders. His counsel speaks across the generations.

Karl Rahner helped me grasp an understanding of two spiritual styles in an apparently casual interview held some years ago. Once upon a time there was a journal called *Herder Korrespondenz,* or *Herder Correspondence,* whose editors, fatefully for my own footnoting, did not print the date of their issues on every page. I have only the evidence, then, of a yellowed, wrinkled, often-folded, and far-faded photocopy. It dates from the days when photocopies were born gray and blurred. The top says "Interview with Karl Rahner" and the bottom, "Concluded on page 645." However, the interview loses nothing because of my inability to cite the issue that was its source or to mark the year in which it was spoken.

9

The interviewer had read Rahner's book *Structural Change in the Church.* "In it you say that one should test one's own faith and spirituality in intellectual solidarity with those who have perhaps excluded God from their horizon." Even translated German sounds Germanic and heavy. "Intellectual solidarity" did not mean that the believer should move to unbelief. It did mean that the unbeliever, the secular person, the modern whose horizon was not open to God, could have some valid experiences. Some of these might readily square with what the believer's heart could also feel. At least, the person of faith could "test" that faith by walking toward a horizon where God has been excluded in the eyes and senses of so many. On that horizon the furious wintry wind blows in the wood.

The interviewer asked, "Is that the point at which the Church of the future can find new motivations?" One pictures the short, stern-looking Rahner, scowling behind his glasses, being deliberate, as always: "Really, I don't know how to answer that question." And then Rahner answered it brilliantly. "I am inclined to think that in the future there will be two types of spirituality and piety—naturally they are related to each other and, once again, are not chemically pure." In matters of faith and piety, nothing is ever chemically pure. The summery types have to be honest and know that behind their smiling façades and their forced Praise the Lords the serious soul knows Absence when doubt pleads for time, when despair intrudes, when death scourges. And what of the wintry persons who test faith in solidarity with those on the godless horizon? They will not endure if they *never* can respond with a Yes. Such seekers will not wait for God forever, unless some warm rays of affirmation break through the winter in their hearts. No, the two types are not "chemically pure."

Rahner spoke of the heated-up type of believer first. He

did not attack this thermal style, but only granted it no monopoly. It "is seen most clearly in the enthusiastic or charismatic movement, such as the Catholic Pentecostals. There is an almost naive belief in the immediacy of God and the power of the Holy Spirit." The theologian verbally crossed his fingers, or bought time: "Whether they are right or not is a question that we can leave aside here—" And the interviewer interrupted him.

To which type should the church give preference? Rahner answered that "in the long run presumably both types are needed." But "from the point of view of pastoral theology and apostolic strategy"—let us say, for the purpose of caring for hearts, or winning them in the first place—"the Church should not place all its hopes in the second [summery] type." Because Rahner was thinking of the people we have pointed to as praising friends, exuberant congregations, or exultant movements, he even warned about their exclusive and shut-in ways. "At the moment there seems to me to be a certain tendency to withdraw once more into the ghetto, and a danger that the Church might try to stake everything on the charismatic-pneumatic movement." Despite his advice, at times it seemed to be the only force that worked, the only product that moved on the market.

Charity marked Karl Rahner's next sentence, and led him to be reserved. Perhaps (he seemed to be scuffing his foot on the floor, shuffling, clearing his throat), perhaps he shouldn't even sound critical at all. Pope Paul VI, and the American bishops, saw in the enthusiastic groups "a new and hopeful sign of the presence of the Holy Spirit." Who was Rahner to counter them? Then came the words of his care: "But the Church has to think more than it has previously done about how to frame its message for men who are troubled, but who in the end have a faith which is certainly not strengthened by a spirituality of the charismatic type."

11

My visit to the wintering heart, this book-length pilgrimage into and through a season that never wholly disappears, devotes itself entirely to the first type of which Rahner spoke. We listen very carefully for the clues this thoughtful man left about this style of search, of gift-receiving.

This type, said Rahner, "would be made up of those who, although they are committed Christians who pray and receive the sacraments, nevertheless find themselves at home in a wintry sort of spirituality, in which they stand alongside the atheist, but obviously without becoming atheists themselves." Atheists, for present purposes, are simply those who "have perhaps excluded God from their horizon." Rahner's winterers regard the same horizon, but they bracket out the atheist's No. They remain tentative. At least there can be a Perhaps, or a Some Day. More than that, since "they are committed Christians who pray and receive the sacraments," some sort of Yes must sustain them on that horizon.

"The Church in its preaching, in its life-style, its spirituality," Rahner advised, must take this type seriously. "To it belong all those who have gone through all the purgatories and hells of modern rationalism." Purgatories and hells! The listener or reader stops short. Modern rationalism was to bring its heavenly cities, not hells. Reason unfettered, people once believed, would lead out beyond horizons where once God had blocked progress. Rationalism was a summer that inspired its own enthusiasm, a sunniness whose rays would lead to exuberance. In laboratories, schools, and societies, restrained people could at least figuratively jump up and down when its freedom would come.

Not so, or at least not *only* so, said Karl Rahner. Rationalism had brought "purgatories and hells" appropriate to the many kinds of hearts that came to know the limits of reason, the loneliness of the godless horizon, the chill of winter with its cry of Absence, Absence. "The Church has to think more

12

than it has previously done about how to frame its message for [people] who are troubled, but who in the end have a faith which is certainly not strengthened by a spirituality of the charismatic type." *In the end:* Rahner is speaking about the Church leaving its searchers on the horizon of godlessness; in the end, these people *have a faith,* nurtured in a particular style.

Rahner has provided a text for our book-length, seasoned meditation. Henceforth the paper on which that text appeared can go back on the shelf or into the file. Let the born-gray photocopy yellow ever more. It can be cherished for the part it played in a decade or two of my development. But now, reprinted on the slightly more durable page of a book, there is some security; less likely will it be lost, now. Better, from this page it may have its influence on others who feel left out from the predominant spiritual strivings and styles but who still in the end have a faith.

PROPHETIC AND MYSTICAL PRAYER

Certain assumptions are in the minds of those who are doomed to, or who readily live with, the wintry style. They cannot make spiritual moves in the century of Holocaust horror or Bangladesh hunger without reckoning, for example: Are those on the horizon of godlessness better reporters, more alert people? Do we who believe somehow, even if weakly, have to live with blinders; do we have to express "bad faith"? Those in intellectual solidarity with atheists are likely to be people who have cried out in anger when God seemed withdrawn, seemed powerless in the face of disease that tore the flesh of a child or parent. They are people who have listened for the Yes when a spouse confronted them with yearslong bewilderments, until in their purgatories and hells they were ready to cry out, "Demonic!"

13

Possessors of the gifts of both spiritual styles, if they are thoughtful, know that over the long course sensitive people have to make sense of their surrounding world. They cannot sustain life in a world that is always and wholly random. A few gifted writers in the Theater of the Absurd, some existentialist novelists, and, it may be, some thoughtless swingers in the condominiums where singles dwell, may have found ways to exist from moment to moment without such sustenance. One can perfect the aesthetic grasp of plotlessness, if there is genius. But even putting a name on chaos limits the chaos. A plot about plotlessness is the first clue to finding a world that is not wholly random. Even the hedonist eventually sleeps off the cocaine or alcohol, or thinks *some* second order of thoughts during the boredom and sadness that can follow the thrill of sexual intercourse. Somewhere there must be connections, clues, plots. Absence, Absence, may be the first, but for few people is it the only, word.

For those where the sacred beckons, where God is a possibility on the horizon, and where the Yes invites or is hinted, more spiritual models than one are now available. In fact, both the summery and the wintry sorts of spirituality come in more styles than one. A great student of prayer in our century, Friedrich Heiler, merits a hearing for the division he drew through both.

"Mystical prayer," one type, "has its roots in the yearning of the devout person for union with the infinite." The exuberant worshiper may not seem to be a mystic in the high and classic style, but she does want to have an immediate sense of the divine Presence. The winterer on the horizon at the edge of godlessness may not seem to be yearning, but an openness in his heart indicates that he is not content to leave church and sacrament and their soft Yes behind.

Heiler also describes another sort: "Prophetic prayer arises from the profound need of the heart and the longing for

14

salvation and grace." The truck driver and the affluent suburbanite who are at home in the charismatic movement may have come there through profound need and longing— both will gladly tell you their routes. But the winterer who finds it impossible to live with their style also has a "longing for salvation and grace."

"Mystical prayer," adds Heiler, is "artificially prepared through a refined psychological technique of meditation." So it is at pentecostal gatherings, where "having the experience" of the Spirit, often taking voice in unrepressed speech called "tongues," results from a refinement of technique. The wintry sort, however, perhaps more common in the history of Christian mysticism, often results from sophisticated modes of meditation. Manuals on these techniques crowd libraries East and West.

In contrast, "the prophetic petition breaks forth spontaneously and violently from the subconscious depths of the religious soul that has been deeply stirred." Again, the summery sorts can know spontaneity. In fact, fervent movements of piety and the spirit advertise their eruptive character. One grows a bit suspicious upon reading the manuals of the movement. They give advice: Start a prayer meeting on time, end on time, prepare the coffee pot for the social hour, discourage the too-enthusiastic pentecostalists from shouting too long or too noisily. Be here each Thursday, read this book. Such advice limits spontaneity, but it does not rule out the premium placed on it. What of the wintry sort, on the horizon where the sense of the sacred is so vague? One hopes that there, too, a person can be "surprised by joy," and is even more ready for violence breaking "from the subconscious depths" of a soul that is not sure whether it is religious or not.

Heiler adds a third distinction: "Mystical prayer is silent contemplative delight; prophetic prayer a passionate crying and groaning, vehement complaining and pleading." Both

styles can know this. Not all the exuberant ones have to talk
or sing all the time. One often reads of the serenity that is
to come when a born-again believer drives her car, or when
another goes about co-parental tasks at the kitchen sink.
There can be silent spaces in such lives. The wintry sort of
person comes less immediately to the point of delight and
may be cautious about using the term or indulging in its
sense, but this one also knows "silent contemplative"
modes.

Both summery and wintry sorts of people, at the same
time, can know the "passionate crying and groaning" of
prophetic prayer. Whoever has visited a joyful charismatic
gathering and then seen someone "smitten in the spirit,"
falling into a swoon, may dismiss the event as being psychologically contrived. It takes little skill or patience, however,
to hear and observe "vehement complaining and pleading"
on the part of one who would be smitten. As for the wintry
sort? There dullness of heart and distance from the divine
may limit the capacity for passion, mute the crying, or
muffle the groans. Given the course of a passage through the
winter of the heart, one will also hear "vehement complaining and pleading." Why does the God on or beyond the
horizon withhold favor? Why does God at best stutter a
barely audible Yes in the hearing of such pleadings?

Fourth, writes Heiler, "mystical prayer is solemn exalta-
tion of the spirit to the highest good; prophetic prayer is
simple outpouring of the heart." Both kinds and sorts can
know both. "Mystical prayer," further, is a "passing out of
oneself, an entering and sinking into the infinite God"; so it
may be on the horizon where the Spirit-filled people dance
and on the horizon where they are in solidarity with the
godless pathfinders through purgatories and hells of modernity. Meanwhile, "prophetic prayer is the utterance of the
profound need that moves the inmost being."

16

Heiler chops sharply; is it too sharply? One more time: "Mystical prayer is a weary climbing by degrees to the heights of vision and union with God." The exuberant spiritist is sure that after the most brief and easy seeking there will be radiant flame and quenchless fire. The more restrained wintry sort of believer is content if only a candle light appears as a signal of God, if there is a tinge of fire to beckon her on during further passage and search. "Prophetic prayer," however, is "a stormy assault upon the Father's heart." The parental heart of God promised care, but seems uncaring. Summery-style prophets storm that heart, expecting it to be open and heated. The winterers among the prophets might storm and storm to find a more distant heart, a smaller opening, a less warm response—but still a response.

THE DISCIPLINE OF THE WINTRY SORT

What separates summer from winter, then, is not mystical versus prophetic prayer. That division survives, though on both sides Rahner would say none is "chemically pure." It is the horizon that matters. The starting point differs. And the starting point for the wintry sort of believer, who never wholly forgets the horizon as it appeared at the start, has seldom received more eloquent treatment than the one the Dutch historian Pieter Geyl gave it as he wrote from his concentration camp. Here is the horizon from which God has been excluded, or from which God chose to be excluded:

> The cold universe,
> Boundless and silent, goes revolving on
> Worlds without end. The grace of God is gone.
> A vast indifference, deadlier than a curse,

17

> Chills our poor globe, which Heaven seemed to nurse
> So fondly. 'Twas God's rainbow when it shone,
> Until we searched. Now, as we count and con
> Gusts of infinity, our hopes disperse. . . .
> God is dead;
> And the sanctuary of man's heart is empty,
> A void place, through which blows a bitter wind,
> Rustling the worn leaves of a lost beauty,
> Stirring the barren twigs of a vanished peace.

I was born in such a setting, agrees the wintry sort of Christian. Or, wherever I was born, in the naive faith and fire: Geyl's words, "cold," "boundless," "silent," "indifference," "deadly," "chills," "gusts," "empty," "void," "bitter," "wind," "barren," roll off the tongue of a person who hurries through poetic passages torn from anthologies of modernity—long books, those—but each can linger in the heart of one who cares to affirm.

Her lawyer says to her, "As we revise the will, let me offer condolences. And, I cannot help but ask as your friend, did your religious faith help you through the crisis? I was not brought up where anything about religion was nurtured or rang true. You were. You believe in God? Was it easy for you? Did that help?" She confesses to herself, as she reads Geyl or hears Rahner, "That's where I live! You are talking about me." And answers: "It wasn't easy. It did help." Another talks to a seatmate on the wide-body jet as they are crowded into numbing and enforced intimacy. The seatmate did not know that a Yes spoken on the landscape of the winterly heart belongs in the community of faith. He had always felt left out, snubbed by the enthusiasts who claimed a monopoly on spirit. He has been on the margins, symbolically excluded. "You speak of Rahner's wintry sort of spirituality?" Yes, you are describing me? Who ministers to me? Does anyone care about this?

At this winterward moment in a passage through the heart's seasons, a moment made concrete in a book, there comes an implied invitation. It is not an invitation to an elite. The wintry sort of spirituality is not the property of a club. If it is expressed at the edges of doubt, this doubt is not to be worn as a badge, as some wear it: "Look, God and people, I am a virtuoso of faith. See me on the tightrope wire, while all the dull clods are smiling forced smiles of Praise-the-Lord faith in their summery landscapes!" If the wintry sort is born on the horizon of despair, despair cannot become fashionable, something to be welcomed by those of masochistic spirit. Members of the club who wear such badges or adopt such fashions might very well reinforce each other until they screen out the possibility of the divine Yes.

The only mark they might come to bear if they stay with the pages inspired by Karl Rahner, if they take this wintry passage, is this: they will not need to feel excluded. They will have seen a monopoly broken, at least in theory. They will, however meagerly, feel addressed. Theirs will not be a visible, defined company. What they seek and what they shall find is not easily marketable. It is not necessarily better or worse than what is marketable and is supported by thousands. They can only claim that their style is appropriate *to them*. Their personalities, makeups, preferences, and searches lead them to this sort of spirituality.

This passage through winter will not indulge those who wish to remain, for reasons of their own, beyond the range of their Yes. The Theater of the Absurdist, who works hard to be consistent, must be a genius to sustain the vision. The existentialist who is rigorous cheats a bit when she fondles her grandchild or is graced by a gesture of love. The walker on the horizon where God is excluded may remember or

19

hope for signals that can well come to the heart open to God. This passage therefore calls for a discipline, whether it leads to strenuous mystical climbings or whether it issues in stabs at the divine heart. If there is a discipline, it implies a tending, a care and carefulness.

In our time, the discipline of the spirit usually borrows its metaphors from space, not time. Most familiar is the journey, the pilgrimage, the way. One begins, walks through, finds company, faces forks in the road, tires, is replenished, and comes within range of the vision of God or reposes in its radiance. All life is lived in space, so the aspect of motion in the passage or journey remains. Whatever else we are, we are bodies that occupy space. Our hearts symbolically move through it.

Karl Rahner's image, however, also impels a movement through time, through a season. Literal winter, we noted, is not the immediate experience of people everywhere: in the tropics, never; in moderate climates, less than half the time. Where literal winter winds blow in the woods, the figurative winter is vivid, sensuously if bitterly alive. But one can read of this wintry style on a summer's day, even in the heat of a desert, and recognize the wintry Absence, Absence, in the heart. Rahner's is a word for all seasons, as transportable to warm seasons and climates as are metaphors of a "journey" or a "pilgrimage" for people in library chairs or at desks.

A caution about the figurative winter is in place. To use it in the context of Christian faith can be jarring, for the image of seasons can imply cycles of life that contradict the Christian movement. Inevitably we shall draw on the remembrance of leaves dropping in the winterward months to signal dying in the heart. Just as naturally our passage will draw on harbingers of spring, as poets and preachers have done with the lilies of Easter, to indicate the other end of that motion. There may be cycles of life in its various passages: from autumn to winter to spring in adolescence, young adulthood, maturity, and age. Or the same passages can occur as metaphors in the movement through crises: before, during, and after divorce or bereavement. The promise of Christian faith, however, is not the promise of cycles, of endless seasons. It knows beginnings and ends. Winter, here, is a dimension of *all* reality, not one-fourth of the spiritual year's endless recurrings.

The wintry sort of spirituality may, at least in rare cases, be pursued the way charismatic Christians go about experiencing their way. A person seeks and may claim immediate contact with God. Its goal is a kind of union with God at God's level. "God talked to me—" "I have a revelation—" "Here is the word of the Lord that came to me by prophecy this evening—" "It is the Lord's will that this happiness should come in the sunshine of your heart—" Gifted geniuses of a wintry sort have also left their pages in the classics of Christian mysticism. They may use other images for their equivalents: the dark night of the soul, the cloud of unknowing, the negative way to God. But they are less likely to be sustained on their lonelier horizon than are the summery, sunny sorts.

2. Texts for the Wintry Way

Can it be only a meagerness of imagination, an impoverish-
ment of spirit, that leads so many of us to get so little out
of "pure" meditation, unsupported prayer? Is the Christian
one who *must* rely upon immediate and direct communion
with God? If so, many seekers will soon grow fainthearted.
Perhaps this point can be most vivid and compelling if for
a moment I turn autobiographical. If "salvation and grace"
depended upon my ability to meditate my way into the
Kingdom, starkly or warmly but without props, the gift
would not likely be mine.

Am I typical? At least at first, barrenness did not result for
want of my trying. After decades of immoderate scholarly
pursuits and moderate activism, often at the side of those
whose horizons excluded God, I found good reasons to be
devoted afresh to the spiritual journey. The mystical chord

has rarely struck: I can count on one hand the number of times in my life that "immediacy" hit me enough to merit my talking about it to the persons closest to me, and can count no times it was worth advertising to the public. Am I, therefore, religiously unmusical? Is faith to be all words and work? Not really, another side of the soul kept pleading: You do have some aesthetic appreciation of Being, of God. You are stirred by the arts, and they demand musicality. They call you to horizons; why should only the horizon toward God find you dulled? Try again, try harder.

The last thing someone on such a journey need feel these years is abandonment. Listings of teachers of meditation fill the Yellow Pages. There are prompters who teach the ways of the soul until one can be unprompted. So far as including "how to" manuals of technique is concerned, libraries on meditation compete with those on sex. A person is taught to borrow from the Buddhist and the Hindu worlds. The Sikh is familiar in the humanities classroom. He beckons with the word that Islamic mysticism has much to offer. Try deep breathing. Purge the mind. Let there be "centering." Think about not thinking about. Then and there may come the Yes, the immediate experience, and all will be well.

Now, fellow winterers can confess to each other that this did not avail: I was soon disturbed because the pure meditative technique did not work. So I would stare at the candle, squinting as the child did until the prisms created by eyelashes made nimbuses—did you, too, see angels' wings in these during long boring church services when you were young? Wearying of that, I might focus on a stone until I had thought of it molecule by molecule and had to move on to the next one in the sanctuary wall. Meditate, the teachers said, so I would let the sun squint through a saint's eye in a stained glass window and reflect with that sun and that eye. To no effect. Meditate, forget distraction; focus on the

23

grain of the sanctuary wood. It was easy to memorize the grain of the wood, but not to find God. Envy those, we were told, who could void the mind of anything that was linear, that pushed forward, so they could be free for the voice or vision of the divine. Saint Anthony did that and was bedeviled. I tried it and had no happy or plaguing demonry; I thought of grocery lists and deadlines.

Feel guilty, advised some teachers and those who successfully meditated. Guilt was a form of immediate experience, however, that also denied itself to this unimaginatively "unguilty" seeker that I was. Where I could not feel, I could acquire experience from those for whom emotion had been vivid. I could draw close by spending hours in a library, whose books told of other means of drawing near the Presence. The library was both a symbol of such means and a means itself. Where did the teachers get their teachings but from texts and libraries? Some thought they were inventing from whole paper their new techniques and visions. They made the mistake of reducing these to print, however, in order to spread and to sell the product. The reviewers quickly noticed: this line was borrowed from Buddhism, this from Saint Teresa of Avila. Here was a technique from Mount Athos, and here one from Catherine of Siena or Margery Kempe. All these paralleled what the books said about Eastern Orthodox Jesus prayers.

At this point, what looked like mere practicality took over. Why bother with a technique that had little promise for me and for my kind? Why try to conjure up guilt where it would not come because it could not come; I knew better than to feel guilty in this case. What mattered was the end of the journey, the effects of the passage in and through wintriness in the heart. The voice and vision of God can come not only immediately, but also mediated. Believers have always known them through words, or what can be encoded in words. They know that words do something to reality. Perhaps they take shape alone when the vital life of the reality to which they point is past. Maybe even the name of "God" encysts what once throbbed in the mind and heart. That word makes possible page one of the book of dogma, and hence, it was believed, enshrined lifeless letters instead of the living spirit. Such an approach, however, undervalues words.

The possibility in texts

In the spiritual search, word and voice can be summons for belief in ways that written words are not. Martin Luther liked to say, for instance, that the church was a "mouth house," not a "pen house." He punned in German that the word should be "geschrieen," shouted, not "geschrieben," written—if there was to be the experience of grace in Jesus Christ. Modern experts on language insist on the difference between *langue,* the systems of language that make books like this possible, and *parole,* the vital word of speech that lies behind them.

Lovers, then, welcome confirming and certifying love letters. These declare and pledge one life to another. She cared enough to sit down and "freeze" a sentiment that the recipient can have thawed after the mail people deliver it. He knows that his letter can be discovered or can survive to embarrass him, and yet he chooses this form to address her. In them is a profound pledge. So course the thoughts in lovers' minds. Few, however, will trade the open, surprising, sometimes shocking words that enliven telephone conversations for something as frozen as letters. When the voice is translated from telephone waves into bodily presence, the quickening between two lovers is most vivid. The text cannot do everything. But it can do some things, and it can do them in special ways.

My address, then, to the needs of the wintry sort of spiritual hearts is based, at rock bottom and boldly, on *texts.* Italicize the word *texts,* and use it again, my notes say, to be sure that no one mistakes the character of this caring. Risk losing attention over something so seemingly banal as a word about texts. Yet the risk can have rewards. Winston Churchill once said that a person can confront a truth a thousand times and not notice it, and on the one thousand and first movement can stumble over it. The reality becomes alive, it reenforces itself. Whether we are here talking about truth is secondary to the fact that we are locating a reality. Wintry sorts of spirituality can find nurture through texts.

Once the splendor of reflection on texts reaches a person, there can be a downgrading of the "immediate experience." At least, it cannot or need not any longer claim a monopoly. The results of both approaches, whether without texts or textually, can be similar. After one comes to that conclusion, the time is at hand for ending frustration over inability to meditate starkly and alone. Good conscience results, even as it charters new work through such pursuit of texts. Maybe these texts are only supports and props at a certain stage in life. One can do without them some day, and engage in free-fall or unroped ascent. Maybe one *need* do without them.

Through texts one can make friends across miles and years. They make possible the stimulation of imagination to picture what it would have been to be someone else, somewhere else, at a different time. In the process, therefore, they allow for an enlargement of personal horizons, an overlapping of my frontiers with those of another in the spirit. One's own soul may be impoverished and thin on resources. The chances are strong that this is so in an epoch of homelessness for the spirit. The text then makes available words from voices in times when divine presence was as vivid as the absence is to a Pieter Geyl today.

What I picture, then, is not a second-rate result but a secondary means of approach. Many images come to mind. Through the text, one can at least for part of the way "hitchhike" on the spiritual experience of another—perhaps a spiritual genius, certainly one more religiously musical than a wintry sort would be. Through access by means of the text, one can "barnacle" oneself to the word of another. One can be a "parasite" that lives off another spiritual organism. These words are not all lovely, not all positive sounding. But the hitchhiker does, or can, "get there." The barnacle enjoys movement, the parasite knows life. More positively: both may be in range of something greater than what they would have known had they stayed home or unattached.

Already by this point a patient and thoughtful reader, someone who is not merely skimming and flipping pages, has gained some sense of what profound texts can do. The poet John Crowe Ransom, on page one, opened the mind to the inner and outer aspects of winter and their conjoinments. Karl Rahner unlocked the door to a treasure by designating two sorts of spirituality. Friedrich Heiler provided what many a reader needed and would not have found by self-centered, voided meditating: two basic kinds of prayer. Pieter Geyl's text froze for many the twentieth-century experience of Absence in a way that a nonpoet without concentration camp hauntings might well have left banal and bland.

This is not a technical text about texts but a reading about wintry sorts of spirituality. Yet even nontechnically, it is unwise for one to hurry past brief comment in broad outlines on what texts do, or can do, or are thought by some scholars to represent. A text by itself "does" nothing. Perhaps it achieves something in the form of a book large enough to serve as a doorstop or for a child to use to turn a regular chair into a high chair. It may achieve a negative result if it is dropped on a toe. A text may be used to line bird cages or to wrap around kitty litter. In the depression, parents made kites out of newspaper texts, but the print was irrelevant if the kite did not tear, but rose a few hundred feet. A text can serve a shredder by being shredded, a recycler, by becoming part of the garbage.

Texts may do such things, or they may do much more. They are, first of all, made up of molecules of ink affixed to atoms of paper. Letters chipped into monuments or raised on coins form texts, and both have their purposes. Ordinarily texts are inert unless something happens, or better, unless someone does something to them or lets them work on the human agent.

To reduce the technical subject to three simple themes, there are certain worlds related to texts. First, say students of texts, they might inspire the interpreter to do what can be done to describe the world *behind* the text. This is a valid, if limited, element in some kinds of literary criticism—though we are not here engaged in literary criticism. That is, one seeks to learn what went into the text. Who was the author, from what world did she write?

In those terms, these chapters have set out to achieve little. True, a line described Karl Rahner as bespectacled and German, but there are plenty of bespectacled Germans who are not interviewed, who leave us no texts on two styles of spirituality. The chapter told almost nothing of John Crowe Ransom, Friedrich Heiler, or Pieter Geyl. One is a poet, one an expert on prayer, another a Dutch historian who—aha! at last, a relevant world behind a text—was in a concentration camp. There Absence, Absence, came easily to the heart. Still, there is not much here to go on to satisfy the biographer's or the historian's impulse.

Unless I misestimate, however, these four peoples' texts worked some effect. They can achieve their effect even if almost nothing of the world behind their texts is available to the reader. How do I know that Karl Rahner is not a hypocrite, talking in bad faith? Some Roman Catholics who ranked this profoundly moderate man as a liberal or a modernizer might think he is a hypocrite. Perhaps he is a Soviet agent assigned to subvert the Catholic faith? Some would say that his counsel makes him sound so: why else ask committed Christians to find "intellectual solidarity" with atheists? I might even have misattributed the quotation. The editors of the *Herder Correspondence* might have garbled things and published an interview with someone else under the name of Karl Rahner. If I find this out, something might happen to understanding, but it is not necessarily devastating. If we find out some day that Roger Bacon *was* Shakespeare, this will not diminish "to be or not to be, that is the question."

Second, one may use the text in the hope of having it match "my" world. This approach sees my world as a neat and finished product. Because it is mine, I can know its boundaries and tend its edges. It is mine to guard, and I can be self-centered and security-conscious about that world of which I am proprietor and inhabitant. It may not be the best of all possible worlds, but at least it is mine.

On some New Year's Eves friends have played a game with one direction and one rule. The direction: pick some other living human being whom you would like to be next year if you were not and could not be you. You have to take on not only the goods but also the bads, not only the assets but also the liabilities, of that person. You might have to be married to her spouse, you will have to die his death, to carry his diseases and bear her limits, even if "being" that person has as a bonus the ownership, for you, of a Nobel Prize. And then comes the rule: you *cannot* be you. Many a party of people who thought they were discontented with themselves and envious of others ended early because so many refused to play the game. They had a world, sometimes a rather rueful one, but at least they knew something of its borders and were content to live with them.

Relatively content in our own world, we naturally tend it. The narcissist does this in the extreme form: where shall I fit this new item of furniture into my already crowded mental furnished apartment, as I like to call my world? The merely selfish person pricks her ears only when a compliment comes her way, or when she is the center of conversation. The person encased in his own world becomes a kind of religious window-shopper or even shoplifter, who acquires only what fits his personal world as it is.

Such an adopter may very well welcome a text. The book on the airport newsstand is designed to cater to his instincts. Here—it leaps out and sells itself—is an address to you as you are, where you are. The reader, of course, always stands the chance of coming to understand possibilities not previously recognized. A text allows for possible modes of being-in-the-world that were not previously present.

Profound texts, classic texts, make the deepest, richest possibilities available. Here we might think of a classic as a book behind which we cannot again get. Once it has been written, published, circulated, and given a chance to make its mark and be cherished in a culture, one cannot imagine the world, its world, without the form of statement that came to potential life in that text. It acquires classic status because of the genius of the author, the appropriateness of the content, and the use to which a culture puts it. Homer, Dante, Shakespeare, Milton, Goethe: authors of texts like these restate and reshape possibility.

Scholars do not know if Homer existed, and some are still not sure that Shakespeare was Shakespeare. Much is known of the worlds of Dante and Milton and Goethe, and their texts disclose much about them. But one need not be engrossed in the biographies of the authors or the social scientific studies of their environments in order for the texts to be effective. The text may disclose to the patient or the startled reader alike various modes of being in the world that had not previously been possible. That world is "the world in front of the text."

Texts do their disclosing best when they are capable of upsetting the reader's world. That is why it is limiting to think of them as merely being relevant to our worlds as we already think of them. Texts that are full of reversals and that most surprise admit an approach that impels one to look for the world that was in front of them. For that reason, many scholars like to restudy and revisit the parables of Jesus. They are upsetting, reversing, and surprising. In them, the smallest becomes largest, the last becomes first, the outsider turns insider, the humblest is exalted at the expense of the proud, the remote gets seated at the head table. This, the reader says, is *not* how things naturally are. Fathers of prodigal sons keep some score on their wanderings, even if in the end they yield to the emotions that welcome their sons home. The parable discloses because it is different from our contemporary experience.

A person who thinks of herself as drawn to or condemned by a wintry sort of spirituality but who does not readily master pure meditation turns, then, to texts. She may wonder who wrote them but, after finding that out, learns that her curiosity is limited or her knowledge confined by certain questions: Was the author sincere? How do we know? What difference does it make, and yet must it not make a difference? Should the author's horizon simply match mine and be imposed on it? She wants more than answers to such questions. There may be in her search something of what Heiler saw in prophetic prayer: an almost violent assault, a ransacking of possibilities. Trivial texts cannot stand up to these needs and demands. Texts must speak from depth to depth.

The seeker will not be content with a text that simply matches his world, but will dismiss out of hand one that does not speak for his experience. The text that addresses a wintry sort of spirituality comes, then, from someone who has passed through its world of meaning, not from someone who scorns or sneers at it. The summery pentecostal or charismatic disdains or dismisses the wintry world. Those who inhabit it are seen as unimaginative at best, or obtusely sinful at worst. They have not prayed, it is said, nor have they admitted the Spirit who knocks at the door of the heart. They do not regard as legitimate or comprehensible any approaches that do not match their own and often have dogmatic reasons for seeing others as "half-safe" or unsaved. The wintry heart speaks to another wintry heart, whether they stand on the horizon beside those who are godless or on the horizon where one does receive a signal, hears a Yes.

The library of classic, if not recent bestselling, Christian piety is rich in such texts. Saints, mystics, scholars, and heroes of faith often acquired classic status because generations with different expectations allowed them to speak out of the integrity of their own experience. In recent, especially affluent cultures, a shift in ways of looking at reality has occurred. In the culture of welfare, for example, a population has acquired a taste for "entitlements." Contrary to the trends of most of the rest of the history of the human race, inhabitants of such culture demand and see their right to basic satisfactions: minimum wages, housing, social security, and the like. These may belong to civil rights. But many people carry over the sense of entitlement into the spiritual realm. Nothing should be denied them. Universe, world, God, they seem to say, you owe me that quick fix, the sunshine in the heart, the readiness to smile. Other experiences are to be denied.

THE CHOICE OF THE PSALMS

If one seeks what we may call a piety for the not naturally pious, then it is necessary to reach for a classic text that goes to the root of the tradition. Without downgrading books on clouds of unknowing or dark nights of the soul, we reach for a corner of the Bible, the Book of Psalms. Not only in that book does the biblical language address itself to the wintry sort. The Book of Job would perhaps be an even more consistent such address. For that matter, the Gospels show the disciples in similar circumstances and styles. Few of them are summery sorts for whom the immediate experience of

God is natural or easy. They are often pictured as obtuse about the signs God would give, slow to learn and see, not easily satisfied spiritually. These Gospels and some dark passages in the Epistles would serve along with many texts from the Hebrew Scriptures that the Christians took into their canon and dubbed, and thus changed into, the Old Testament.

The psalms have the clearest claim, however, for any spirituality based in the Hebrew and Christian traditions. Why the psalms? Certainly they are accessible. If a Gideon Bible in a hotel room or on an airplane has been used at all, it is likely to flop open to the central pages of the psalms. These hundred and fifty Hebrew poems, most of them sacred and some of them secular-sounding, have been adopted by Christians. They inform many New Testament songs, and early Christians sang them at worship. "The church's prayer book" or "hymn book," many call the collection. In a way, the psalms are a plotless anthology, but their mishmash and absence of sequence do not disturb the faithful who use them. If any portion of the Old Testament gets bound with the New for slim Christian pockets, it will be the psalms.

They are not all and only for corporate worship, making up the church's book when that church is gathered. Where families held devotions, the psalms came to be part of the vocabulary of the children. Memorizers memorized them, for many phrases stick, and deserve to stick, in the mind. Hardened urbanites, far removed from the nomadic or agrarian experience, turn in crisis to those who minister to them and ask for a psalm about the Lord as Shepherd. Why? Because they resonate to a passage about walking through the valley of the shadow of death. Moralists use the moralizing psalms to teach reflection on the divine law. Sampler sewers stitch their phrases into samplers and hang them on

34

the wall, as did their grandmothers before them. In the stark
night watches of the dying, some have followed the discipline of reading a psalm each night. Travelers far removed
who want to think of home agree to number their days apart
by reading a psalm each day. Like smooth coins, the psalms
can lose their ability to be felt. They give off few rubbings,
especially if one selects among them and seizes the familiar
in order to make them match a given world.

As for the pilgrim's use, it is clear at once that one cannot
know much of "the world behind the text." Whereas once
upon a time the Church confidently assigned these or those
psalms to, say, King David, modern scholarship has led even
the conservative away from a secure linking of ancient
psalms with titles and descriptions. No one knows who
wrote them. Seldom do they give sufficient clues about their
environments for anyone to identify clearly the events that
inspired them or to which they refer. Decades ago, scholars
were sure that this or that psalm was used at a coronation
or an enthronement, but their heirs are more cautious. The
giant scholars of the psalms boldly classified them into
types, *Gattungen*, but these did not turn out, in Rahner's
language, to be "chemically pure" either, and now have
fallen into disuse. One can suggest that they appeared over
several centuries' time on the soil that today we call Israel.
They had much to do with the temple cult, and some were
designed for royal use. But the common person is given a
voice in them, too.

If the world behind the text is not easily available (yet still
the psalms speak), neither can one find a simple match between the world of the psalms and our contemporary world.
For the most part they are not simply relevant, they do not
line up with ordinary experience. Where they are summery
and enthusiastic, they are so with an ease and unselfcon-
sciousness that make modern imitations sound forced.

35

Where they are wintry, bleak, and restrained, they carry one to depths that normal people resist, and feel they ought to resist. Most people who have read them thoughtfully in sequence, for example one per day, report on barren days when nothing in that day's psalm spoke to them. These passages evoke enemies who have or should have no modern counterparts. Many are royal and we are, or call ourselves, democratic. They are rich in rural imagery but the rural is now remote for most. God is near in the summery psalms in ways that few experience the immediacy of today, or remote in the wintry ones to the point of denial and threat.

We are left, then, with the world in front of the psalms, where their reversals and surprises occur. How in the midst of a sunny-dispositioned psalm can we make sense of an absolutely bleak descent into the abyss? And what makes possible a word, *any* word, of trust, in a psalm that begins in the slime and mire of abyss and envisions an end in a shadowy Sheol, where the dead, given no voice to praise the Lord, receive no ear bent toward them in the eternal silence? And yet one trusts, one praises. How, and why, and toward what end? Whoever follows such phrases and assumes some consistency will find that other possible modes of being-in-the-world offer themselves. For that reason the psalms might startle the modern reader and motivate a "fusing of horizons." That is why someone who seeks what Rahner calls intellectual solidarity with those on godless horizons can possibly hear the first Yes on those horizons, given the open world of the psalmists.

To use the psalms for a spiritual search is not to need or write a commentary. The commentary is a thoroughly legitimate means of scholarly access to a text. In its academic mode, it will do what it can to inform the world behind the text. Massive books describe what earlier scholars proposed about settings, terms, intentions of psalms. In its preacherly mode, a commentary will make connections and point to relevances, so an ancient world can become intelligible. A commentary ordinarily is a disciplined, line-for-line expounding of a text, usually following some sequence. Commentaries, however, are not the only legitimate parallel texts. Some of the greatest and most helpful books on ancient texts have a different goal and means. These books ransack and plunder old texts, tear them apart and reassemble them, sometimes superimpose their interpretations and at other times merely listen. The act of taking the text thus apart and rearranging it in the light of some norm or other may free one to explore the world in front of the particular text.

A fictive reincarnate psalmist might come on the scene and legitimately complain, "That's not exactly what I meant with that line or stanza!" At the same time, one could argue that an author does not have complete command of a text even on the day it is written. It is a creation; it is not the author; just as a piece of pottery acquires a shape and life that neither matches the bodily proportions of the potter nor embodies all the ideas, including all the ideas of Pothood or This Pot that the maker might have. "Did I say that?" one sometimes asks of a line in a letter of promise. Yes, one did, truly, but without knowing it was said.

An assemblage of psalmists, be they committees of singers and choirmasters or tormented lonely poets, would not recognize their work in the almost random sequence in the Bible. Only the first psalm seems intended to be located where it was, an introduction to them all, though many scholars discern psalms that seem to have been written or chosen to end sections of the book. Yet the melange and mix of Psalms did come to be gathered into the Hebrew canon. The Christian church took it over. This canon has come to us in a package deal, as it were. Users of it know that it has acquired an aura and a sanctity comparable to the halo and holiness that the very stones of a chapel sanctified by use and prayer might have. Readers range through this canonical collection sometimes purposefully and sometimes as if on a rambling stroll—just as they move through life and its journeys. The psalms: the word evokes a memory-impression of a whole body of literature. It is that body, that canon, that has before it a world whose horizon invites explorers.

In this canonical use, the reader is constantly if not overtly asking: What is it about the community that created these hymns that speak to us, and what did this, its creation, do to keep changing the community—even as it can change me in my community today? In such a use, the psalms call more for response than for expounding. They are often stereotyped, in some cases almost embarrassingly so. They domesticate terror and grief. Just as often, the feelings that they transcribe from the heart and voice to parchment and page are raw, unfinished, full of hooks that will catch the modern reader. Sometimes they are violent, offensive, indefensible: who can allow for reversals in which God will honor those who bash the heads of enemies' children against the walls? At other times they break themselves open and offer a jewel we do not deserve or understand. At all times, since they came in an arbitrary order, we may reorder them to new purposes. They are used as triggers for fresh thinking, not as agents to close off thought or experience.

Of course, integrity, the integrity of the modern reflector and of the book itself, demands that one do not do simple violence to the psalms. An honest person listens patiently, is informed by scholarship. History, says this historian, matters. Ethics demands faithfulness and fairness where issues of history arise. The poetry has cadences that should not be disregarded. The cubist painter had a right to rework planes of guitars and vases, but his act had to be overt. The composer, be it a Charles Ives or a Gustav Mahler, who quotes other music and changes it for purposes of irony or the sardonic, telegraphs what he is about and does not parade the borrowing as authentic reproduction. The ransacker, nevertheless, does some sort of complex violence to a text, especially if that act can startle one into views and visions that were previously hidden.

Through recent years of ransacking and personal plundering, something occurred in my reading that made me associate the psalms with Rahner's wintry sort of spirituality. So in notebooks that grew up not on my scholarly desk—as a student of the modern era I have to plead that the psalms "do not belong to my period" of research—but from bedside, sickroom, or island and desert reading, I began to take notice. Is this psalm more appropriate to the summery or wintry, the sunny or the windswept spirituality? The commentaries could have made the notetaking easy, since they classify dozens of these psalms simply as "laments." The line was not so easy to draw, however, since many laments were not written at the horizon shared with the godless. They were written as laments on the edge of simply affirmative experiences in the face of a God who is near, and benign.

To my surprise I noticed that more than half of the psalms had as their major burden or context life on the wintry landscape of the heart. Many more contained extensive reference to the spiritual terrain of winter, even if it did not predominate. Only about a third of the psalms were, indeed, the simple property of those for whom the summery style would exhaust Christian spirituality.

Such a reading and notetaking led to a challenge that sounds more belligerent than it is intended to be. Those who think that Praise the Lord defines the only Christian landscape, that the smile must be ever present and that, for the reborn, joy should always come easily, have to show that what follows is a consistent misreading. Or they have to reject the classic text of Christian devotion, the psalms. Or they might adjust their natural piety to make room for the apparently less natural piety of today, one that must have been common in the centuries of the psalms.

This reading of selected phrases from selected psalms, then, is a kind of invitation to a shared experience. Those who find the summery Yes and the Christian answer easily available no matter what will, I hope, find a growing empathy for those who by personality and in faith are their fellow Christians but who cannot live where they do emotionally. Those who have felt neglected by the predominant literature and set of ministries, if these confine themselves to the ease of sunny piety, might not find here a complete address to their situation. They might nevertheless find from it some readings that can help them on the first steps of their journey. They come from someone on a horizon near where the godless live, but who remains a committed Christian. That person reads texts of others who have horizons where the summer sun does little warming, but who also do not lose trust. Instead they build trust, and for that reason they startle, they lead to reversals, they disclose modes of being that are so unfamiliar they might help save us.

3. The Slanting Toward Solstice

IMPATIENCE WITH THE TRIVIAL

Some years ago a famous man died and was buried. The
"and was buried" suggests the measure of pomp appropriate
to the well-off and the important. He also was a public man
of no recognizable faith. His family and friends comman-
deered an under-used but reminiscently appropriate college
chapel for the occasion.

The powerful and the rich were present. Lacking a book
of rites and ceremonies, those who sponsored the service did
what moderns do: they invented a nice little liturgy of their
own. Several bleak songs by a near-contemporary composer
were the only sounds verging on anything sacral that participants heard. They were also treated to numerous—
some remember ten—eulogies. As is the case with many
eulogies of those on the horizon where God is excluded, or
goes unremembered, these more often described the world

41

of the speakers than of the one spoken of. The congregation learned what Speaker A had meant to one dimension of the deceased and what Speaker D meant to two others. We learned of the administrative, anecdotal, scholarly, and charitable activities of the departed. All this took place without an amplifying system to make all parts of the service audible. The event occurred before the chapel was air-conditioned. The elite people of the city melted pounds away in the steam and fumed away other pounds in discontent over the muffled sounds.

At the end of the unbearably long service, a well-traveled and well-heeled urban patriarch reached for the arm of a young clerical friend. "You'll be around long enough to take care of me, since I am near the biblical age of threescore years and ten. Promise me one thing. Dredge up from my past the Book of Common Prayer. Have them dig a hole for me. Put my body in it. Read Psalm 90 over the grave. Lower the casket, throw on the dust, and let that be it!"

Years may have passed since the man who gave that prescription had lived familiarly with the prayer book or Psalm 90. But now in an hour of dire, even desperate, need, he was trying to find an alternative to the plotless service he had just barely endured. The old words came back. He still loved a text known for its beauty and realism. For his end, there need be no self-glorying eulogies in a freshly patented Order of Service.

Those who knew the old man well could have surmised that he would have little taste for any cleric who might enter his circle after his death and give his bereaved family some glib answers to the Why of his departing. His choice would be a counselor who might simply come in and share the sacrament of the coffee pot through the long night with the widow. They might sit in silence together while the two tried to make sense of a loss. Maybe the man was self-assured enough to guess that the widow might not be inconsolable in the first place. Her late husband could in that case be dispatched without undue emotion. In any instance, he trusted classic words, spoken out of realism to realism. These were words honored by usage, read from black books over gaping graves through centuries in many climates. Psalm 90 would do it all for him again, as it had done for so many others before his generation.

THE THEME OF TRANSIENCE

Psalm 90 is the classic psalm for the winterward mood. To think in the figures of seasons, it is one that leans from late Indian summer toward the inevitable solstice. A journey through the passage of a life marked as a year reaches a point where leaves fallen and grass withered signal demise. The solstice has not quite yet come. So far only flurries of snow have dusted the corners of the porch. The chill has caused citizens to pull up their coats around their necks; they have not yet reached for their mufflers and gloves. Warm days still intersperse themselves with the cold ones, so an illusion of potential moderation continues. It is only illusion. The warmth will soon go. The pin oak leaflets still cling though all the other leaves have dropped. The last charring from the burned leaves of grass emits a bittersweet odor. Soon even that will go.

The cadences spoken at many a grave, as signs of death to come, use both the times of day leading to night, and the sense of seasons, the cut grass, leaning to winter. "Thou turnest man back into dust" (90:3), "for in thy sight a thousand years are as yesterday; a night-watch passes, and thou hast cut them off; they are like a dream at daybreak, they fade like grass which springs up with the morning but when evening comes is parched and withered" (90:4–6). No sun remains on the daybreak landscape. Winter is coming and the leaves, faded, will burn. Fashionable therapies or do-it-yourself techniques to make everything come out right are pointless now.

The end of the psalm still does offer an extension of Indian summer. It does not seem to grow naturally from the rest of the psalm: "May all delightful things be ours, O Lord our God" (90:17). That line is for the summery sort. In its recall there comes to mind a cartoon in which two men visit in a bar. One, a Mr. Polyanna, rattles off to the other something to the effect that "I had a happy childhood, a happy adolescence, a happy adulthood, and now I have a happy old age, and then I want to go straight to heaven." Just so simply the psalmist wants "all delightful things," as if he were a child again.

Such a late verse might sustain a person momentarily as he reflects on dust, cut and parched grass, and readings over graves. It has little to do with the realism of the psalm in general. "All our days go by under the shadow of thy wrath; our years die away like a murmur" (90:9). The ancients knew that sound waves stop and leave no retrievable trace. The echo and overtones prolong them, but they do not long put off the end. They become muffled, muted, and fall silent, as does a life.

One does not need the text of Psalm 90 to have an experience of the sort that Psalm 90 illumines. It comes at three in the morning when a person feels alone. A bedmate, if there is one, sleeps, ignoring the sense of Absence, Absence. The awakened partner hears the little minute-plaques tumble in the digital clock. A drip comes from the bath. Now and then a floor creaks as the house adjusts to the cool of early morning. The years die like a murmur, and the sounds one year has made will be forgotten with those of the million years before.

Tomorrow, the roused one thinks, I will make better use of my hours: "Teach us to order our days rightly" (90:12). For now, what is there to do but stir, go to the bathroom or the refrigerator, stroll aimlessly past the window to see the deserted street, and retire again? Next morning all that remains from the waking is a remembered sense of the brevity and the smallness of life. "Satisfy us with thy love when morning breaks, that we may sing for joy and be glad all our days" (90:14). Even that prayer sounds like a bid for one more good time before the bad, one extra day of Indian summer before the inevitable closing of the door on life, the closing in of dirt over dust. The sun of the closing verses is out of place. It has little to do with the evening tone of the rest of the psalm. Who remembers the gladness of the end? Psalm 90 leaves only dust.

THE CLOSED-IN SENSE

Transience: no word better capsules what the winterward sides of the year and its match in the human heart signal. A second text, Psalm 39, is another address to this issue, again with its sense that an end is impending. A reader can still reflect and make plans in the light of its themes. This psalm is not the word of an unengaged philosopher who enjoys the classroom luxury of speaking about how brief life is. The psalmist writes with a sense that life has become a long diminuendo. Having observed the parade, he has heard the trumpets. Now only the muffled footsteps remain at the lower end of the avenue. Each step of the marchers is softer than the one before. The flourishes are past. The listener recognizes this also "close to home." This canvass of his own cells and members speaks more clearly than would books of philosophy. He looks for shelter in the face of hopelessness.

The sense of wintriness grows as the reader finds the

45

psalmist locating no hope in personal achievements. Relying on his accomplishments made sense back when he was still in the market for books on what self-improvement might do for him. Now he is past the age of being an agent.

Twice the psalm that he reads draws its imagery from the weather that marks the season. "Man, though he stands upright, is but a puff of wind, he moves like a phantom" (39:5–6). Being a Hebrew poet, the author has a right to repeat himself, and he evidently liked the phrase: "Indeed man is only a puff of wind" (39:11). The psalm line is in mind as the person looks at the snowscape where the first dustings have fallen. No great blizzard force is needed to move the snow, no noteworthy drift occurs. A more quick zephyr comes from nowhere, whisks the flakes, drops them away, and leaves no other trace. This, says the writer, is what I am like—and, now, the finger points to the reader: you are, too.

At first reading, this kind of psalm threatens to deaden human efforts. Any efforts designed to result in prosperity are doomed: "The riches he piles up are no more than vapour, he does not know who will enjoy them" (39:6). Who will? His widow? Children-in-law who did nothing to earn the reward and who never will become responsible stewards? If he cannot pass his accumulations on to his own bloodline, then why should he bother with endeavor? "All his charm festers and drains away" (39:11).

In recent years some conservative Christians have made scapegoats of "secular humanists," the people Karl Rahner found at that horizon where God is excluded. Their scapegoat, however, is a luxury. The believer also wants to enjoy achievement, but religious faith includes such a strong sense of death that humanists will rightfully question whether the religious can make a contribution to life.

A typical witness is Frederick Olafson, who discusses the

enterprise of the humanities: "The relationship between humanism and religious belief," he writes, "is one that has given difficulties for centuries and has caused a good deal of personal anguish. . . ."

> There have been forms of religious belief that are radically incompatible with humanism because they proclaim the nothingness of man and transfer to their gods every possible form of agency or achievement with which man might otherwise be tempted to credit himself. . . .

Then Olafson tempers himself, knowing that not all is lost:

> But there are also religions that teach that there is something, however limited, that human beings as individuals and as societies can do and that thus concede a measure of significance and value to the achievements of human culture and even allow a modicum of human pride, as well as of shame, stemming from the contemplation of what has been done.

The author of Psalm 39 seems to have the worst of both worlds. Many commentators say that he could at least have had the pleasures of faith if his sense of an afterlife—a bright spring after the winters of life—had been vivid. It was not. So he was left with a denial of the validity of the human venture. It is a puff of wind; that is all. Yet he had no escape beyond life. So why bother with God?

A wintry sort of spirituality commits a participant in the journey to traversing the terrain with psalmists who do not, frankly, promote a consistent or vivid notion of an afterlife. The Christian, conditioned by readings in the New Testament, is likely to be shocked when she marks with an underlining pencil the very few psalmic passages where any kind of life beyond the grave offers comfort or promise.

Even the closed-in sense that goes with transience makes the wintry horizon plausible. Curiously, the idea of a second life seems to be less of a motivator than one might expect. Among peasants in the Middle Ages, the historic athletes and heroes for God, and martyrs to be sure, have endured unimaginable sufferings because of their sense that these will be compensated for in the life to come. Yet Marxists overplay their case when they claim that the promise of afterlife is the only motivation for bearing with evil in this life. The psalmist was pleading not for a second life but for meaning in this one. If God is God, these texts suggest, then there should be value already to our days as they pass, but there seems to be all too little. Charm festers and drains away, who lives to enjoy riches? And wind twice puffs as winter advances.

It all turns on the character of God

So far one can follow this kind of writing as if it were itself merely an example of humanism. The genre belongs to "vanity" literature, a form in which any secular author can indulge. A dramatist in the Theater of the Absurd could be at home with the testimony as far as we have carried it until now. Thus far no "world in front of this text" jostles a person on that horizon where God is excluded, simply because in so many ways it matches the world that nature brings. This all amounts more to a wintry sort of *life*, but not of *spirituality*. These psalms position the reader at the side of the atheist efficiently enough. Their viewpoint, however, coincides with that of the atheist. Rahner's "still committed" believer makes no appearance. No reversal occurs. Nothing startling discloses itself.

The psalm, on closer reading, however, *does* belong to the history of spirituality and not to that of vanity. Some turns in it leave one restless, en route to a possible peace. They instill the impulse for the winter journey in the sight of a leading, living God. Otherwise, what do we make of this: "And now, Lord, what do I wait for? My hope is in thee" (39:7). The first half of that line leaves one apparently abandoned; the seeker no longer can put a name on the content of hope. Yet a believer always hopes *for*, hopes *in*, hopes *that* —and never merely hopes. Then, with a wonderful suddenness and no sense of logic or continuity at all in the second half of the line—is it not this way that the Presence is disclosed?—he says, "My hope is in thee." The second affirmation comes with an image that responds to the climate and the weather: "For I find shelter with thee" (39:12).

Everything here turns, then, on the character of the living God. This Presence on the horizon differentiates wintry

49

spirituality from mere wintriness. A fugitive story—I can no longer trace it—tells of two men on a several-day fishing vacation. "What is your wife doing tonight?" asks one. "I haven't the faintest idea." "What? How can you trust her, if you don't know where she is or what she's doing?" The second one mumbles that he is not curious. He feels no need to snoop on her; he has confidence.

The first questioner is not content. He has to cite chapter and verse of their relationship to show on what his trust is built. "Oh, I want to be able to have confidence in my wife. I know exactly what all her moves are. When I ducked into the general store for a phone call, I was checking. Last night I saw to it that she would be playing bridge in a foursome with your wife, so I could check that out when I got back. I know that tomorrow will be her club night. I have friends who'll report whether she was there. There's no room for fooling around. I know her movements and that's why I can trust her."

The man to whom he addresses the question is speechless. He has no words to go with such a concept of trust. To be inventing continual tests, to be enduringly suspicious, to want to check up: these are precisely what trust is not.

The second fisherman places his confidence in the character of the trustworthy spouse. She has a record on which he can rely. He knows of her integrity. She is, intrinsically and through her love for him, predisposed to be trustworthy. The trust can grow precisely because the two do not and did not have to check up on each other. "My hope is in thee." There are no secondary rationales, no props, no scaffoldings. Nor is there even a promise that the hoped-in one will make an exemption and spirit the believer away from a world in which the snow puffed by breezelets outlasts the winterer. To counter the claims of the summery types, the realism of the psalm returns in its last line. After a request for a smile from the Lord, there falls the deadening "before I go away and cease to be." *Before I cease to be.* Any Yes the psalmist speaks has to be uttered in the face of that starkness. In the wood, a furious wind was blowing. We are left with the puzzle of that startling position that allows for a void—"What do I hope for?"—and a completely confident hope.

The earth slants more as the season passes, and the heart chills with it. After the puff of wind comes the blizzard. Transience finds its successor in the coldness of death. Hope, far from being confident, becomes a hope against hope.

4. Spirit at the Solstice

A WINTRY HEART: A "BEING TOWARD DEATH"

Winter, the season when a pole of the earth slants farthest from the sun, finds the shadows longest at noon. Somewhere around December twenty-first in the northern hemisphere, or June twenty-first in the southern, the tilt is greatest. The long chill begins. Before that time, in the moderate climates, some snow will have fallen to follow the dropping of leaves, but the illusions of postponement can be extended. The slant, the tilt, the time of solstice mean the end of illusion: winter has arrived.

Winter is more than dormancy: it is a dying. Poets who have springtime in view make much of the way the earth needs annual sleep. Animals hibernate. Trees rest to draw strength for a new bursting of buds. Nature is quiet, but will become vital again. Poets are also beings who are aware of standing on a horizon that opens toward death. The leaves that have dropped from the living trees will never return. Though at first the smell of their decay was sweet, it turned acrid. In the dryness of late autumn, they disintegrated. The twigs are gone. No poetry or wishing will return them. Though some animals will revive from winter's sleep, others have gone to their caves as to their graves. They disappear, and when spring comes the wanderer ponders: What happened to all the carcasses? Where are the dry bones?

A wintry sort of spirituality does not literally trace the cycles of the seasons and is not a weather report or an observation on the climate. This spirituality treats winter as a metaphor or an image of the heart and soul. The wintry image, because it represents more than dormancy—death—forces an urgent theme on the spiritual seeker. The search for a piety does not permit evasion of the central issue of life: its "being toward death." Every Yes hereafter has to be made in the face of "ceasing to be," as the world ordinarily knows being.

The wintry sort of spirituality, says Karl Rahner, promotes solidarity with those whose horizon excludes God. For those who are serious about this, excluding the mystery of death is the great determiner of their distance. Awareness of a probable "ceasing to be" and inability to say Yes in the face of it combine to lead them away from any desire to reckon with God. Whoever says "God" has chosen to imply goodness and power. If there is goodness and power, why is there death or the pain and suffering usually associated with it? Did God cause the death? If so, where is goodness and love? Did God have the power to abolish death and not use the power? That version advances nothing, for where, even then, is goodness and love? The third option seems hardly more attractive. It holds that God may be powerless to work life in the face of natural death. Why bother with a God too weak to create and sustain what matters most to every person? The questions will not be suppressed.

Committed Christians who fuse horizons with those of the godless know they cannot evade the questions. Attempts to smuggle the reverent unbeliever into the kingdom by calling her an "anonymous Christian," as Karl Rahner would, meets with opposition. The resisters say, in effect, "Don't baptize me with terminology where you cannot reach me with water."

A classic illustration of this was when some French Dominicans came to admire the writings and character of the novelist Albert Camus. They wanted to find ways to include him anonymously in their camp but found him drawing back. Finally he addressed them, inviting dialogue. They should remain Catholic and he agnostic, he said, staying in their separate camps. If Camus could make sense of a God who permitted babies to die, he could find the Christian scheme attractive. Since he could not, their faith remained fundamentally unattractive, whatever lesser benefits it might bring.

Not often do believers have the opportunity to engage those beyond their own horizon that includes God, the way those Dominicans encountered Camus. In recent generations the nonbelieving community has tended serenely to ignore the claims of faith. When they see evidence in the media of a commercialized and trivial entertainment business in the name of faith, the creatively godless shrug their shoulders. They have better things to do than to pay heed to such voices and options. These mean no more to them than would popular astrology to most Christians. Entertaining Christianity, though it employs a language that includes death, is in a hurry to pass over the Good Friday story in order to reach Easter. Such a diversion does not allow the reality of death to loom.

Summery-spirited Christians know that they will have to

die along with everyone else. The resurrection of Jesus Christ from the dead, since it took the sting out of death, in their eyes, removes some of the seriousness of death. Mentions of rewards for the graced life after death are frequent, but seldom is there a walking through the stages that lead to death. Since much summery Christianity concentrates on healing, it must bring up the fact of disease. Here again, however, the theme can be trivialized, because in the popular books or on the television programs, one comes to meet only with the success stories. People throw their crutches away; the cancer cells miraculously disperse; life is prolonged. Well and good, think those of the wintry sort, but prolonging does not do away with it. Death remains. The leaves fall, decay, and disappear. The heart knows, and demands a listening to its confusion.

Believers who find themselves at home with the wintry sort have been so voiceless that those who exclude God from their horizon are hardly aware of those who hold to faith. When the believing community begins to produce realists on the subject of death, people who take it seriously on their own terms, their act occasions surprise.

DEATH AND THE STAGES OF LIFE

The theme of death reaches people differently in various phases of their lives. Young people given to wintry sorts of spirituality will not and should not find themselves focusing on it. Father John Dunne of the University of Notre Dame found this question to be a human constant: "Since I must die, how shall I satisfy my desire to live?" He noticed that the question comes in a new way to people in around the fourth decade of their life. Young people have probably been close to someone who died. We are told that they will have seen eighteen thousand violent deaths on television before they reach college age. Such ritualizing of violence, however, screens real death from view and makes it easier to evade.

Death up close is not a present reality for most of the young in a modern society. The architecture of housing cooperates: there is no upstairs room for grandma in the ranch home, no corner for grandfather in the apartment or condominium. If a member of the senior generation dies, the grandchild is at a distance. After death, the body of the elder is usually disguised by the cosmetic aspects of the funeral parlor art. Only professionals are physically near the dying: the cleric, the medical staff, the funeral parlor director. Even they find safeguards against having to make death personal: they can pull screens and use sanitation and monitoring devices to keep the dirtiness of death distant. Busy calendars and schedules remove the opportunities for reflection, and there is even new terminology to shroud the realistic language about death. Once upon a time people died in community, but now they die alone. All this has a bearing on death for the dying one, but it also changes the nature of the surviving community.

An author writes lines like these as if with a kind of automatic impulse. He fears that they will seem lifeless because they have been repeated so often. Yet he must move one step further and risk more repetition by entering into the present record the observation that death is supposed to have become a taboo subject. A yawn comes easily when one hears one more time that in the nineteenth century sex was taboo and death was a popular subject, whereas in the twentieth everyone can talk about sex, and almost no one brings up death. Recently there has been some change in this context, and books on death have sometimes even become best-sellers. Seminars on the subject attract wide notice. Still, Christian parish leaders report that however voguish the topic may be, it does not attract audiences or readerships that have any staying power.

Even where the talk about death and dying comes with ease, a certain taming of the subject occurs. Many a therapist can rattle off the "stages of death and dying" as outlined by Dr. Elisabeth Kübler-Ross or her competitors or successors. To put a name on stages, however, does something to make them more domestic and safe. Such naming is a part of therapy; why criticize the healing impulse? What a culture gains in therapy it may lose in its grasp of soul. Death has its own power. It also resists being graded, located between strata of life or seen following neat stages. Death comes with the brutal crash of steel as autos meet on freeways, through the quiet slit of steel with a razor at the wrist, with the thieving suddenness of a coronary occlusion, with the silent stealth of infant crib death, with the adding-machine efficiency of genocide, or with the plotlessness of invisible mass killings in Kampuchea. The naming of stages does little to prepare a person for the many ways that the last enemy uses to attack.

John Dunne found from reading spiritual biographies that somewhere around age twenty-nine or thirty profound people pass to a new stage of awareness. They appropriate the horizon that death creates. People who have watched television death for entertainment or who have read objectively about dying begin seeing subtle changes in their own bearing. They have begun their new move toward autumn. Doors close, options narrow. By now they have been fated to follow one vocation instead of another. They have vowed to spend life with this mate and not that one. As they mature, they hear the commentators describe athletes or mathematicians of their age as being "over the hill." Through the centuries, cultures and the dictates of the body have worked similar effects on diverse people. They move from observing death at a distance to reckoning with its possibility close at hand. Some of the deep religious experiences of conversion occur at about that time. The journals of spirituality, especially those of a wintry sort, start to be written at that age.

If Dunne is reckoning correctly, the age when people take death seriously as a personal reality, a point that today occurs before midlife, was near the end of the average life span for people in the ancient world. If the psalms are to serve as a text that discloses a creative way of being in the face of death, it is important for a reader to remember how close death was to everyone in the original context of the book. No actuaries kept statistics on the people of the era. Through complex means of calculation there can now be educated guesses. The young person of today can expect to reach Psalm 90's minimum of "threescore years and ten." When the psalms were written, few could look ahead so far. In ancient Greece and Rome the average span was believed to be just over twenty years, in medieval England about thirty-three. Two centuries ago it had risen only to thirty-six.

WANTING ONLY GOD IN THE FACE OF DEATH

In the psalms, all views of death had to reflect its closeness. The earthy naturalness of Old Testament stories reveals the nearness of death through battles, floods, accidents, miraculous disasters, or any number of other causes. Death was both a part of nature taken for granted and a punishment for evil, the result of God's activity. To make sense of the psalmic attitudes toward death, it is important to set a larger Old Testament context.

The writers of the psalms confronted death but saw through it to life because in death they saw God. This notion seems startling because the psalms have so little to say in general and nothing concrete to say about a positive mode of being in afterlife. Sheol, the abode of the dead, was attractive neither to visit nor to take up residence in. Sheol allowed for no visitors, and none ever returned from it. This shadowy world was, and in retrospect is, a horror without mitigation. The language of winter is too serene for Sheol's miry, murky landscape. And yet, one must say, despite the language of "ceasing to be" or going to Sheol, there is a Yes in the face of such language in the depth of Hebrew piety.

One angle of vision comes from subsequent styles of Judaism. Two lines from eastern European eighteenth-century Hasidic Judaism reflect the long afterglow of this vision.

Rabbi Zalman, one of the great successors to Hasidism's founder, the Baal Shem Tov, was said to have interrupted his prayers to say of the Lord: "I do not want your paradise. I do not want your coming world. I want you, and you only." This was in the spirit of his predecessor, who said, "If I love God, what need have I of a coming world?" Such language is not likely to satisfy moderns who wish a more open future. It is an important first word for those who have only utilitarian views of God. In the world of the practical, God is loved for the sake of one's self, for the self's purposes, and for the yield of this relation in the reward of eternal life. The ancient Hebrew loved God for the sake of a long life in which to enjoy creation, but she also was to love the Lord for the Lord's sake.

The Christian tradition in its vital years picked up something of this sense of the love of God and of trust in the divine ways wherever they lead. From the tradition of Bernard of Clairvaux in the Middle Ages there survives the story of a woman seen in a vision. She was carrying a pitcher and a torch. Why these? With the pitcher she would quench the fires of hell, and with the torch she would burn the pleasures of heaven. After these were gone, people would be able to love God for God's sake. Here, as so often in Hebrew

59

thought, a regard for the *intrinsic* character of God and of divine trustworthiness shines through. A believer shifts away from a bartering concept in which one loves God for the sake of a transaction. Now there is a relation in which the trusting one is simply reposed in the divine will. The journey through the season after solstice in the heart will take on purpose and become bearable.

The Hebrew Scriptures from page one prepare the seeker for such an embodiment of God. Genesis asserts that God antedates the beginnings. The Scriptures have room for two different creation stories on the first two pages and for others in the Wisdom Literature, in Job 38–39, and elsewhere. No one can collate these stories in order to deduce a scientific account of how the world began; the texts have a different purpose. While some religions have no interest in beginnings, faith within the Hebrew Scriptures insists that the Creator is the Lord of all that follows—including death. Wonder over the universe of nature is a derived wonder. Such awe exists not for its own sake but because God is the agent. The world and the holy as such, the seasons of weather and the heart as such, are not of intrinsic but of derived value. Everything depends on trust in the Creator.

Death as defined in a sacral world

Whereas this understanding was all very comforting to the Hebrew who had such a vivid sense of the Creator's presence, it seems to do little to help believers and unbelievers comprehend each other's horizons. It does little good to talk about those horizons until a reader has done more justice to what the psalmists thought were his own. Today the world is described as "desacralized." For many this means that the universe has lost its innate sacrality. No longer has it a native capability to generate transcendence and inspire awe. Today humans set out to control the rivers and oceans, the resources under the earth, and the seasons themselves. The Hebrew's world, however, was sacralized not because of its innate and native character but because it belonged to God.

God's world included human mortality. According to the Eden stories, death came as a punishment for disobedience. More than disobedience was nevertheless involved. Death was the marking line drawn between the divine and the human, between created people and the Creator God. Adam and Eve chose to strive to be immortal and to have knowledge. These both belonged only to God, who would have given creatures one but not both of them. People became mortal, but they had knowledge. This knowledge is what inspired the Hebrew drama and reflects itself in the psalms. People now do not live to be immortal, but they have knowledge. Death, therefore, though a punishment, is also a simple fact that defines the creature over against the living God. The human now knows something of "good and evil," life and death. Eden meant ignorant immortality. After Eden comes informed mortality.

The psalms frequently remember that death is a punishment for disobedience, but more often they are matter-of-fact, and the punishment idea is lessened. Responsibility for living replaces the consciousness of punishment. Humans are not to be beasts, nor to live like beasts, for they are still in dumbness, in ignorance. The knowledge of death, for all the grimness of realism it introduces to life, is what gives daily and yearly existence meaning. Humans no longer have immortality, but they have history, memory, and hope. Remembering is the root of trust, hoping is the center of faith.

Although Sheol is a threat with whose horrendousness we moderns cannot cope, death itself in the psalms is not *mere* enemy. God does not act like an Oriental potentate who enjoys humans, like puppies, tumbling before his throne until it suits a divine whim to have them killed. Death, indeed, is not the result of a whim but is to define what is human. Astonishingly, then, in this concept, death is not simply evil any more than winter is evil in the passing of the year. Death is not a reality designed to call humans to refuse the enjoyment of living. Death, the definer, gives meaning to life and history. It is an instrument that helps provide meaning for daily existence.

To the psalmists, death is not an instrument that acts on its own. God controls death and uses it to reinvest history with meaning for all people who live in its presence. Many biographies in the Hebrew Scriptures need be only as long as a modern *Who's Who* entry. We seem to "know" vastly more about these ancient persons there described, however, than we do about accessible moderns whose lives can be summarized in reference to the clubs they have joined, the awards they have won, the children they have sired. Part of our knowing about the Hebrews comes from the way these biographies round out. Simply: "And she died." Death was not only a depriver, as it was for many other people. It was not even a tragedy in the conventional sense, however sad it may be for the mourning survivors. The Hebrews who survived, let it be said, certainly did mourn.

One searches the psalms and the whole Hebrew Scriptures futilely to find the equivalent of an encyclopedia article of the sort that could wear a caption, "Death, Biblical Views of." Never does a writer stop short and say, in effect, "In order to present our views of life and of God, we now have to take up the topic of death." The relative isolation of the theme into a particular chapter, as in this book, is unknown. Death comes up in the story of the lives of David and Job and Moses, just as winter comes up in any account of a year.

A moment ago we noted that the Hebrews mourned. The stories of mourning are themselves classics, just as they have been models for later people. One thing never happens in them: There is no equivalent of a consoling cleric who enters the room of mourners late at night to give pat answers to the question, "Why?" There are no palliatives, no explanations of the sort that bumper-stickers condense into a phrase such as "Christ is the Answer." Death has simply spoken. Its word about what defines the human is final; there is nothing more to be said. Scrolls, little black books, embalming fluid, nice little liturgies, morticians, poetic eulogies—not one of these could conceivably serve to create illusions. The living make no contact with the dead, and they dare not aspire to. They have to shift their affections to survivors, for the dead cannot feel them or reciprocate them.

THE IMPULSE TO BELIEVE IN FACE OF THE THREAT OF DEATH

Each believing Hebrew had to learn what their literature imparts to later readers. The texts teach the intrinsic value of each day. They turn mourning into a regard for the living, not for the dead, who are beyond reach. With this goes a reality that confirms our sense that a wintry sort of spirituality dominates these Scriptures. The living are all also beings who appear on a horizon toward death. No matter how righteous they may be, not everything turns out well for them in life. The psalms often do focus on a "Why?" That is inspired by whatever it is that limits meaning in the life of the righteous who must die, *before* they are on the verge of dying. So limited and immediately confining seemed the language of response to the Why that some later rabbis came up with equivalents to the Christian belief in the resurrection of the body. They needed "immortality" to compensate for what limited them in this life.

In the rabbinic versions of immortality, God finally evens accounts for the righteous. Among other things, they can resume relations that they had known on earth. The scriptures are never very clear, however, about such reunions. Jacob does not expect to meet his missing and presumed-dead son, Joseph. Sheol is a zone of darkness and chaos in which such a meeting would be meaningless, indeed impossible. Sheol is thus no match for Greek or later rabbinic immortality or Christian resurrection. The Hebrew Scriptures have no language of bliss after life. They give no voice to a hope for a creation that is reflected back into the old world, thanks to the values of life after death. Sheol follows life but does not serve as an afterlife. It has been said that Sheol is better seen as an after*death*. Sheol never makes its appearance for comfort, to inspire a different mode of living now. Afterdeath is a winter from which no spring emerges, after which no summer invites.

Because the Hebrews of the type who wrote the psalms concentrated on the trustworthiness of God and not on the gift of afterlife, they did not ask for more living after death. They pleaded with God as the giver of life to endow the meaning of their seasons with value. Seldom do they stand in the divine marketplace and bargain for a life to come, though some do haggle for more years. God as the Lord of life matters more than their ego and their survival.

Even to record such conclusions of biblical scholars may contribute to the wintry chill that reaches many corners of the texts. God simply keeps asking creatures questions that admit of no easy answer. These impel them into full and busy lives in the light of a divine purpose whose extent remains finally unknowable. Unknowability does not in the end mean silence. God, who is personal, addresses humans and expects response. The drama of daily living results from that conversation.

Later Judaism could not leave things so wintry. The Talmud quotes a rabbi: "The end purpose of everything our Mishna has described is the life of the world to come." The motive of the rabbis was less to elaborate on the sketchy traces of belief in afterlife within the Bible than to make sense of their faith in the justice of God. God, they thought, *had* to do more than the Scriptures revealed, in order to even out the injustices of this world.

Such rabbinic notions introduce a springtime. The psalms leave those who pray them with a winter radiated by awareness of the divine power over both death and life. The rabbinic teaching on immortality that tempered the psalmic faith began to offer an escape from death by an escape after death. Jewish messianism, because it proposed a purpose to future history, also qualified the old faith of psalmists in the trustworthiness of a God who also made each day meaningful on its own terms.

After centuries of rabbinic teaching on immortality, Jewish faith in messianism, and Christian witness to the resurrection, it is hard to pull the screen back down to cloud the future as the psalms did. Moderns reflect on the past as if all people in it faced death with equanimity because they believed in recompense in a life to come. That belief appeared in the interval between the era of the psalms and our own. Faith in a life to come has by now disappeared from the consciousness of many. They live under the confining canopy of their unguided years. Novelist John Updike (in *The New Yorker* of January 11, 1982, p. 95) refers to this interval "when death was assumed to be a gateway to the afterlife and therefore not qualitatively different from the other adventures and rites of passage that befall a soul. . . . Most men until modern times prepared for and enacted their own dying" with a sense of calm, even matter-of-factness. Somehow Updike implies an affirmation in writing that at best says, "Blackness is not all."

Blackness of winter night dominates much of modern

literature and consciousness. Lacking both faith in an after-life and trust in a Lord of life, those who exclude God from their temporal horizon are left then only with the pain, never with value or meaning. Updike cites an example from a diarylike novel by Lars Gustafsson, *The Death of a Beekeeper,* to suggest the measure of pain. This journal records the last days of a Swedish beekeeper who, as he is dying of cancer in 1974, isolates himself in his beloved cottage. The novel is at home with wintriness:

> It was gray, pleasant February weather, fairly cold and hence not too damp, and the whole landscape looked like a pencil sketch. I don't know why I like it so much. It is pretty barren and yet I never get tired of moving about in it.

Such prose could be translated back into the language of psalms, which also allow for at homeness in a bleak land-scape. The diary, however, records the winter night, the pain without relief. One can only enter the novel by reading into it a prolongation of the brief stabs and piercings that almost everyone has had momentarily in, say, the dentist's chair. Can we find a God worthy of trust on this horizon?

> What I have experienced today during the late night and in the early hours of the morning, *I simply could not have considered possible.* It was absolutely foreign, white hot and totally overpowering. I am trying to breathe very slowly, but as long as it continues, even this breathing, which at least in some very abstract fashion is supposed to help me distinguish between the physical pain and the panic, is an almost overpowering exertion. . . .

The reader imagines herself in such a winter night, without promise of relief, without a responsive God to break the silence:

The reader imagines herself in such a winter night, without promise of relief, without a responsive God to break the silence:

> This white hot pain, naturally, is basically nothing but a precise measure of the forces which hold this body together. It is a precise measure of the force which has made my existence possible. Death and life are actually MONSTROUS things.

Death *and* life become monstrous because dying is monstrous. Death is no longer the divider from God that defines humanness, life, and thus the good. A sufferer is left with mere breathing to divide and define pain and panic.

A summery faith of the exuberant sort moves rapidly past such pages. Self-help philosophies address other aspects of life. They not only fall silent in the face of such pain but refuse to hear the cries of pain uttered. On such terms, sunny styles of religion cannot serve as a basis for any solidarity of experience with those whose horizon excludes God. On that horizon, nevertheless, is a faithful reporting of the human condition.

THE PURPOSE OF STARK TEXTS

Is there a wintry sort of spirituality, or is there just a wintry sort of personality or philosophy? As one embarks on a reading of the psalms in pursuit of the world in front of their text, a legitimate question is, "Why bother?" What advantages are there in a spirituality that traverses such a bleak landscape? What is wrong with illusion, evasion, escape, and the keeping up of appearances by the avoidance of death? No complete immediate answer is possible. No answer will be fully satisfying, except one that suggests an intrinsic value in the act of facing up honestly to the limits of the human condition. A partial answer, however, suggests already that if a reader is to find a Yes disclosed in the wintry psalms, she cannot find it without first feeling the arctic winds from their landscape of death reaching her as they did the ancient Hebrews.

The psalm that reflects the mood of soul-solstice beyond all others is Psalm 88. "The world before the text" in this unique case is a wintry landscape of unrelieved bleakness. The psalm is a scandal to anyone who isolates it from the biblical canon, a pain to anyone who must bear it apart from more lively words. Whoever devises from the Scriptures a philosophy in which everything turns out right has to begin by tearing out this page of the volume. Its lines suggest a frozen Niagara Falls, a stalactitic maze of frozen drops forming a curtain to defeat the seeker on a spiritual journey.

Readers who are familiar with the summer of thanksgiving psalms have made numerous efforts to place this one in relief. Maybe, some suggest, something went wrong with the producing and transmitting of many biblical texts. Scholars believe that the last page may have been lost from the manuscripts of Mark's Gospel. After the resurrection story, instead of closing with something cheering and triumphant the Gospel ends, "they said nothing to any one, for they were afraid." So it could be with this psalm. Many gloomy ones end with something of a benediction, a squint of hope. Could it be that somewhere through the years before the scribes became protective, a page was lost? The text, however, appears to have an integrity in its present form.

We are not likely to find a scrap of millennia-old parchment to pretty up this psalm with a happy ending. We can

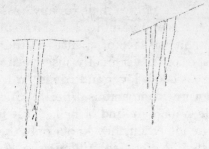

nevertheless make a virtue of the necessity of its absence. Assume that what is here is what was intended to be here. The seeker of spiritual discipline cannot be satisfied with honing, sanding, and smoothing until a text becomes inoffensive and fits without abrasion. What part does such a text play in the search of a believer who can accept it as it is? At the very least, it can be a test of the endurance for those on the journey who wish to proceed through a stark winter in order to see how the reality of God and the fact of trust can emerge.

On those terms, a crisp, quick witness crosses the mind: the people who let a biblical canon take shape were never interested in glossing over unpleasant realities. They had no sense of modern public relations. They showed no interest in making their product palatable. The writers and collectors were moved by a love of their God and an impulse to promote praise and faith. Yet they let angular, misfit pieces of poetry like Psalm 88 speak to and for them. This psalm, then, can serve to moderate less harsh ones. A person who comes in from below zero weather to a temperature slightly above freezing knows there is comparative warmth. The inclusion of this text is a sign of the stamina and boldness of the psalmists and their anthologists.

Can we look, as we always shall, for any Yes? The nearest one comes—and it is important for those who undertake the agony of prayer in the face of silence—is the form of the address. The speaker never finally loses relation with the Thou. "Thou hast taken lover and friend far from me, and parted me from my companions" (88:18). Such abandonment by people is its own kind of hell. Those in woe often benefit from friends when they know only the absence of God. The depriver, in any case, still merits a "Thou." Three times an "O Lord" sounds as a pained and staccato accompaniment of the plea. A universe without the Thou seems to be a Siberia of barrenness. Those who live in such an empty universe can employ no language but a shout. They have no place to direct it. A motive here remains to keep the conversation going: "O Lord, my God, by day I call for help, by night I cry aloud in thy presence" (88:1).

Through it all, then, God remains the agent of living and dying. The times remain in God's hands. The Thou seems to have a cruel tinge, for the woes are not the result of natural forces but of the work of this God. "Thou hast plunged me into the lowest abyss, in dark places, in the depths" (88:6). God has also "made me loathsome" to my friends (88:8). No hint of human responsibility for the circumstance appears. God alone caused the troubles.

The consistent images here are not simply compatible with our analogues to a wintry climate. They employ the language of physical illness, and they may reflect such illness. If the beekeeper of the novel had found God addressable, he could have converted his language of pain into something comparable. We read of "my fill of woes," of being "like a man who lies dead," and "beyond help." The "loathsome" appearance could have been a literal reference to disease. "I have suffered from boyhood and come near to

70

death; I have borne thy terrors, I cower beneath thy blows" (88:15). The lines reflect no momentary lapse in a loving relationship, but a trauma of long years.

Now it is time to face head-on the reality of Sheol. This occurs not by visiting its physical landscape in the dream of the mind, but by picturing its effects. The woes "have brought me to the threshold of Sheol." The writer goes "down to the abyss." This is not a place of mere mud and the vapors of slime and shadows. Sheol is worst when it spells the end of relations. I "have become like a man beyond help" (88:4). Lying dead and sleeping in the grave, the one who prays feels abandoned: He is the one "whom thou rememberest no more because they are cut off from thy care" (88:5).

If this were the only line of the only surviving psalm, especially if the Thou of "O Lord" were lost, we could know no possibility of God on the wintry horizon. By installing death as a boundary and committing humans to have a history, however, God created a presence through history. If the Creator places people into Sheol to forget them and cut them off, only life "in dark places, in the depths" remains. In this winter night there is no star, no candle, no fire through the cottage window for refuge, no false dawn, no dawn coming at all.

The rabbis had a difficult task when they witnessed to immortality in order to show God being just. The psalmist here knows nothing of it and expects negative answers to questions: "Dost thou work wonders for the dead? Shall their company rise up and praise thee? Will they speak of thy faithful love in the grave, of thy sure help in the place of Destruction? Will thy wonders be known in the dark, thy victories in the land of oblivion?" (88:10–12). No, and no, and no, and no are the implied answers to all four questions.

The only chance for God to show a relation and expect a
response at the time of writing must occur this side of the
grave. Only the wan "O Lord" keeps any tie alive. Better off
the animals, dumb and unremembering, not knowing, immortal for all they know and care.

The world in front of this text almost collapses into the
world of those who exclude God from their horizon. The
line of difference is finally reduced to nothing but an "O
Lord." Almost nothing of practical worth seems to come out
of a difference so trivial. Karl Rahner, who provided our
theme, was interested in those who for all their solidarity
with such godless victims of the modern landscape, kept
their faith. If this psalm is to stand alone, we are speaking
not of solidarity but of identity: godless and godly are in
practice seen as one and the same.

How minister to the impulse to escape the mere abyss of
Sheol, or the unrelieved winter of our metaphor? Is there
some glimmer of light in the dark, some glow to anticipate
the spring? The best I can do is the thought of a canon. This
is not the only psalm. Nothing can carry us further in its
direction, but there are other directions and other psalms.
What use shall the believer make of it? Here is one: when
misfortune comes to believers, those who stand outside their
circle expect faith to disappear because it must have been
born of illusion. They presume that no thinking person
would have believed had there been no assurance that trust
would bring exemption from the terrible. Believers, it is said,
get a comeuppance for their ignorance because they never
anticipated ill fate.

The world in front of the texts in the whole canon allows
for summer and noon. The canon is never a book of compro-
mises where everything evens off in balance. Whoever has
followed the disciplines of spiritual pursuit and scriptural
reading has already stared at the depths. If this psalm does

not dispel illusions, then no message of realistic hope can reach the believer. At this point of solstice this small comfort has to suffice.

DEATH AS PUNISHMENT FOR SIN

Some relief begins to come from psalms that connect death with punishment for sin. Although they do not settle the natural questions as to why there is a universe in which God helps people become accountable in these psalms, there is at least a sense that the victim could have done something about the circumstance. Psalm 38, much of which is as unrelieved as Psalm 88, has this aspect. "Thy indignation has left no part of my body unscarred; there is no health in my whole frame," but now it is "because of my sin" (38:3). Iniquities are a heavy load. "My wounds fester and stink because of my folly" (38:5). To gain some sense of how far we have traversed the winter landscape, it is startling to picture that we begin to think of this as a beginning of affirmation. The psalmist or the empathic reader has become partially an agent, not merely a victim.

The abandonment by other humans remains consistent, as in the other psalm. Friends and companions shun the sinner, and kinsfolk keep far away. As so often in the psalms, gossips make things worse. "Those who wish me dead defame me, those who mean to injure me spread cruel gossip and mutter slanders all day long" (38:12). The description of woes is consistent as well. There is scarring, festering, stinking; loins burn with fever and wholesome flesh is gone. Commentators rush for relief. If in Psalm 88 they could think that a page might be missing, in Psalm 38 scholars can observe that the talk of woes has turned into patterns and stereotypes. No one in the psalmist's condition, they argue, could create, recite, or write such agonies. Therefore this

73

must be a kind of all-purpose, index-carded lament. That coded character mutes its rage and violence.

Greater relief begins to sustain the searcher as the worst of winter's first instant has passed. In this psalm a window opens on hope. The world of possibilities in front of this text jostles a believer with the suddenness of an apparently unmotivated interruption: "On thee, O Lord, I fix my hope; thou wilt answer, O Lord my God" (38:15). No answer from God yet guarantees a summery "everything will be all right in the end." Instead, an answer appears at this point to be nothing more than continuing relation. Yes, God may step in to be of saving help. Maybe taunting enemies will then be silenced. That is small comfort compared to the greater one: God may not break off the acts of responding. The psalmist even takes steps to develop the bond with God, chiefly by regretting wrongdoing which has helped separate him from God. In the end, a note of desperate but creative urgency comes through: "Hasten to my help, O Lord my salvation" (38:22).

THE FIRST PROMISE OF RESCUE

Sometimes enough warmth suffuses these wintry psalms that one can reckon with the thought of rescue. To sustain the winterer through a bleak landscape still to come, it is valid to reflect on a psalm that speaks in the past tense of rescue. To do so is to keep as a problem for another day the fact that there will be problems for other days. In Psalm 30, Sheol can be postponed, if not averted: "O Lord, thou hast brought me up from Sheol and saved my life as I was sinking into the abyss" (30:3). The psalmist does not write in complacency. The author is aware of having contributed to what we might call a near miss. "Carefree as I was, I had said, 'I can never be shaken' " (30:6). As always, God remains the agent of contingency and change: "But, Lord, it was thy will to shake my mountain refuge" (30:7).

A grim note of something like gallows humor comes at the edge of this psalm. It takes the form of an urgent conversation between victim and agent, created and creator. "I pleaded with thee, Lord, for mercy: 'What profit in my death if I go down into the pit? Can the dust confess thee or proclaim thy truth?' " (30:8–9). Here is almost an echo of the God created by the trust of the human, sardonically represented by poet Rainer Maria Rilke: "What will you do, God, if I die?" Psalm 30 pictures God fulfilled by praise. If Sheol removes a person from divine hearing, then to relegate her to that realm is to reduce the cohort of a cheering section by one.

The metaphor for winter serves well here because it suggests how a bracing jolt can awaken anyone who is complacent. This psalm describes how the writer had fallen into a condition that in the Middle Ages went by the name of *acedia*. This referred to an inability to shake the demon of noonday, to respond in any way except by sadness in the face of spiritual good. The spiritual life can be nickeled and dimed to death, it can disappear as in death by freezing.

Although at the onset an approach to death by freezing stings, the later stages are supposed to be almost pleasant. At first one feels a guillotining of fingers, toes, and nose in the arctic night. Later, as the winterer stumbles on, a drowsiness begins to occur, say those who have barely escaped such death. The journeyer becomes complacent. Even the snowbank takes on the guise of a warm and inviting blanket. I will succumb and repose there! To succumb and repose invites death. The style of living for this psalmist had been listless. Carefreeness had meant carelessness. It took awareness of death and a final separation from God to induce care and response.

Psalm 30 is a night song, appropriate for the modern pilgrim who has drifted into false security. It is for those who enjoy fastness or carelessness in the name of carefreeness. Perhaps the ancients sang it in a temple vigil when night came, but today lonely worshipers also find it congenial. The psalm anticipates a better time. The psalmist has known such seasons: "Thou hast turned my laments into dancing; thou hast stripped off my sackcloth and clothed me with joy" (30:11). As hours pass, "Tears may linger at nightfall, but joy comes in the morning" (30:5).

To one who operates outside the rhythms of this psalm, who brings the logic of persistent questions, this is not a permanent easing. The laments have been turned into dancing because of past rescue, but what of the future? The sackcloth is gone, but will it not again be in place? Joy comes in the morning, but there will be another night. Night has the last word, in the form of death. If one followed such logic, Rahner's "committed Christian" would not survive the experience of winter shared with the godless. Nor would the grand theme of the wintry psalms come clear. The believer who prays them is not fundamentally a bargainer in a market transaction. She is not one who loves God for the sake of an afterlife. Aware of the meaning of afterdeath, the psalmist focuses entirely on the character of the God who inspires hope against hope, trust this side of Sheol. This promise, the winter wind still blows in the heart and soul.

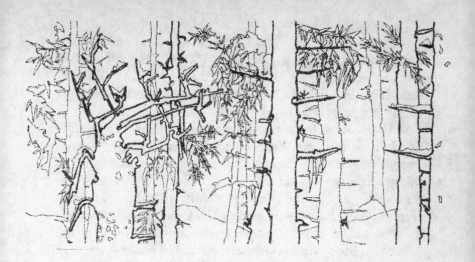

5. The Enemy in the Dead of Winter

The solstice with its sunslant and longest shadows is not the worst of the cold. The time of chill has not yet had its full effect. During the months of slow return toward equinox, the winds in wintry climates have their chance to blow most furiously. Midwinter follows, the season in which plants exposed to weather suffer winterkill.

This death of plants has analogies within the heart. There, furies of the forces around impinge on the soul and threaten it first with coldness and then with death itself. The lyricists who voiced the psalms were perfectly capable of looking within themselves to find many sources of the chill and absence. Notable among these were the sins that merited punishment, the disobediences that evoked divine wrath, the errancies that provoked reaction. These failed responsibilities they coupled with the simply natural fact of death

77

under the plan of the divine agent of time. The winterkill of outside forces in their eyes produced a kind of compensatory rage. It could block out thought of access to God or response to the access of God in the soul.

In the psalms, the outside agent appears most frequently under a code name, "the enemy." The "enemy," "foe," "enemies," "foes"—these words make over a hundred and thirty appearances, almost one per psalm! Because of the dominating role of the enemy in casting a shadow or forcing response, a reader has to cope with this figure. Unless the modern seeker comes to terms with this reality, it is not likely that the positive spiritual force of the psalms can work its effect. The world in front of the text opens the reader to modes of being that include an encounter with inimical forces.

THE THREAT IS REAL FOR ALL

Let me step momentarily into the role of the typical reader. This half-fictive "I" speaks for the author, and could speak for many readers as well. I: this character does not simply identify with the psalmist when he makes the most desperate moves in the face of the enemy. This I has a spiritual life that has been largely unmarked by any awareness of forces or persons who are about to do me in or who have already conquered. I am, of course, not naive about human nature. Realism is not alien to my experience. No one can be a historian or a reporter without being able to cite the whole litany of modern theological statements about raging humanity. Some of these statements, because they are so crude, have an almost biblical brunt: "People are no damn good." "The sons of bitches are gaining on us." As all-purpose philosophies of life they often work.

The mystery of why evil seems built into the structure

and pattern of ordinary events is a spiritual problem. Why do the righteous suffer? This question erupts willy-nilly in the heart. Psalms force it, and that creates trouble. Why do innocent children die and beloved spouses drop over with heart attacks? Why do responsible mid-career employees lose jobs, well-nurtured children rebel, and spouses turn icy? Questions like these lead to doubt about divine purpose. If God is God, how can these things happen? If God is good, why does God not prevent their happening? Ageless questions, easily turned banal because people voice them so often, they are as readily enlivened with bitter force whenever one realizes that the answers are as remote as ever.

A wintry sort of spirituality calls people on the journey to walk on the bleak landscape with those who have excluded God from their horizon on these very grounds. The deniers act both by instinct and through intelligence. You can feel the unfairness of life in the bones, and you can reason your way to see it if eyes are open and minds are clear. Have lunch with a philosopher of popular psychology and self-help. You can see that she does aid some people in forming positive mental attitudes that enhance a personality. The result is better sales and advancements in career. You ask: "Does your philosophy always work?" Yes. "Does it help people in all circumstances." Of course. "Are there no problems beyond its range?" No.

For a moment an illusion creates its alluring web and invites you to come in. Her success stories are beguiling. Who would deny them, or find a good reason to? Better a bright mental attitude than a nightly half bottle of Scotch to exorcise the demons. Better self-help thinking and resulting success than failure or, even worse, than wallowing in failure. No special divine purpose is served by the awareness of human indignity. Nothing in the biblical concepts of humility inspire self-hate or any absence of self-worth. Therefore,

A Cry of Absence

to hear a philosopher of worth describe an all-purpose outlook, one with happy endings for all who employ it, there are good reasons to lean forward in hope, to listen. Maybe, at last, someone does have a handle with which to solve the question of human misery. You ask your lunchmate: "Do you really mean that there are *no* circumstances that your philosophy does not address, *no* contexts in which people will not have problems solved if they follow you?" She answers, without missing a turn of her spoon in the cup: "I mean exactly that."

The luncheon conversation with the self-help counselor may vividly bring to mind recent newspaper stories. They refer to events among people remote from local experience. Such people, of course, do not count for as much as Western Europeans or North Americans. Still, an item on page 8 can anchor itself in the mind and remain there to attack at surprising moments and undercut optimism.

Because the stories come to us chiefly through statistics, their force is blunted. Thus 10,000 are swept away by a tidal wave churned up by the Indian Ocean on an Indian shore. Another 6,000 are killed or missing in a Turkish or an Italian earthquake. Reports have 150,000 starving in Uganda, or the Sudan, or—where was that spot on the African map? These all, generally, result from natural forces over which forecasters or planners have no control, defenders no defense. They simply happened in the course of nature. They left the defenseless dead. What, you ask, does your philosophy have to say to that?

The smiling philosopher across the table does not rattle her luncheon teacup. She loses no beat of rhythm in the stirring with her spoon. She sweeps her hair back on the left side, leans back, and with a self-assured gesture says, "Now you are changing the rules of the game. I am not writing and lecturing for Bangladesh and the Sudan. My market and my constituency are reasonably well-off Americans who have not lived up to their potential. Is there something wrong with helping them?" Nothing is wrong, you agree, no, nothing at all. Now *she* is changing the rules of the game. You two were not talking about marketing a philosophy to a select strand of humanity. You were pursuing all-purpose philosophies of life, inclusive addresses to the human condition.

The psalms speak frequently to the questions of Why as these are based in natural disaster or as they have to do with misfortune based on human irresponsibility. They do not answer the larger Why. Their answers do not eliminate disaster or lead one to shrug off responsibility. The psalm reader who would walk in the faith of these ancient texts has to reckon with the problem of divine distance, passivity, or loss of control alongside the problems that rise because of faith in the divine controlling of history and death. In awe over the scope of the psalmists' claims, "I" can easily identify with all of that.

A sudden shift in the issue of responsibility for troubles comes in the dead of the wintry heart. For the psalmist, the killers are the constant enemy or enemies. To this I, the enemy is an infrequent villain, an alien in the cast of characters. Good fortune, says the reader, has protected me from direct assaults by enemies. In my decades, no foreign military force has challenged my nation's shores. A welfare state with its social securities protects my entitlements. When these become insecure, no single enemy is at fault. It is hard to read the international oil-producing cartels into a role in the psalms. Why make spiritual problems of legislators who have honest political differences over economic policies that threaten my security?

In vocational life, from time to time enemies may appear.

Someone on an office staff or team finds me *de trop,* which means she wishes me abolished from the human race. If I am inefficient, she resents my inability to meet deadlines and to clear my work slate. If I am efficient, he is envious of the dispatch with which my agenda clears, or he is put off by my productivity. I cannot win, and am cornered. A trip to the water cooler or the washroom becomes a jeopardized pilgrimage. The track seems land-mined, the walls booby-trapped. We meet: she turns a shoulder, he averts a gaze. Either can force invention of a circuitous route past many desks so I do not have to come face-to-face with the persons who wish I did not exist.

THE PREOCCUPYING OPPOSITION

What appears at first to be a mere inconvenience based on a psychological quirk gradually takes on the dimensions of spiritual threat. Though the assault is trivial, the response to it is demanding. I must summon inordinate energies to out-flank or outwit the in-house enemy. Before long, I begin to fret, to lose sleep, to engage in melancholy soliloquies on the way to and from work. I open my homework, and my mind wanders. I seek resort in the psalms and find the passages that once opened the Spirit to me are now blocked by preoc-cupation. Strangely, the more trivial the enmity I feel, the more confusing and demanding are its claims.

In response, this threatened "I" tries to keep perspective. On a faculty one has enemies. Indeed, academic life makes room for foes on a proverbially grand scale. Trench warfare seems moderate compared to the gatherings at the trough for the meager rewards a modern college or university has to disburse. The gatherers are trained by their disciplines to disguise their greed under the terms of altruism and humanism. A faculty, after all, fights over tenure because that system assures academic freedom. The battle may be over departmental autonomy, because that system keeps the disciplines away from amateur meddlers. Right? Whoever intrudes on policies affecting these patterns violates human learning. He had better be exiled.

After a sequence of faculty committee meetings, I seek perspective. Suddenly one occurs: Here we are, fighting as if all human destiny awaited the outcome. Yet over one enemy's shoulder a window opens on the Chemistry Building. That second foe has a back toward a window fronting on the Law School. The room with its four sides has space for one more enemy; she backs on a window toward Social Sciences. Beyond the three windows, then, are three buildings. Within each, a committee is fighting as we are. Then this comes to mind: In six decades of using this building for academic fighting, not one decision we made has affected chemistry or law or sociology, to say nothing of affecting Washington or Warsaw or Wall Street. None of the enemies in the buildings two hundred feet away ever threatened or advanced the world of those within ours.

Both the realization that most enemies I know represent safe or even trivial causes and the perspective that sees history little altered by them are helpful in the spiritual quest. I become free again to go seek out the deepest texts and to let their worlds shape my own. A clarifying, balancing thought comes to mind: my autobiography would include more friends than enemies. I have always been surrounded by people who were secure enough to be able to spread security, free enough to be free and to promote freedom. Is this circumstance fate, luck, unmerited grace, or an achievement that these friends and I have worked for? We can postpone the answer while relishing the reality; friends, not enemies, predominate in many vocations. That fact makes it difficult to identify with the psalmist and his hundred and thirty scenes written in the face of an enemy.

I, this typical I who has so far escaped the worst of human enmity, can easily use this protected experience to turn into a Pollyanna or a Pangloss. To do so would be to rule out in advance the possibility that the world in front of the psalm text is closed off for me today. Such foreclosure could be dangerous. Psalms about the enemy are securely in the canon, and presumably they have spoken to countless hearts. To dismiss them because of a sheltered vocation and immeasurable luck might be an act that needs a word of the New Testament: let the one who thinks she is standing be heedful lest she fall. The enemies strike stealthily, and aim particularly at those who have enjoyed a record of protection and shelter.

Before I take the victims of enemies seriously, however, I try one last ploy. Let me dismiss the psalmists as paranoids. Everyone knows that a certain personality disorder leads people to overimagine the threat of enemies. Something in their being, their childhood development, or later mental illness or accidental experience, causes them to magnify the slights they feel. What the healthy can dismiss as mere heedlessness on the part of others paranoid persons enlarge into uncontrollable anxiety. In confidence, they report each morning on fantasies and nightmares, in which their enemies, all of them ghoulish, figure large. They build up stores of anger that they must somehow work off, one hopes nonviolently and without destroying supposed or real enemies.

"Take them to psychiatrists." Well and good, one says of this counsel; but then you also have to take along the writers of these psalms. They then also sound paranoid, unduly anxious about threats. They sound angered to white heat. They are ready to expose those enemies to winterkill.

JOINING THE HUMAN RACE

After refusing or being unable to dismiss those reports on lives lived in the face of an enemy, the previously sheltered person can make another use of the world opened by the psalms. He can join the human race. While some may not have had an enemy at hand, and while others stand mute or dumb in the face of overwhelming natural disaster, in every generation millions *do* find it possible to cry out against winterkill in the heart because of forces or people around them.

Violent images of enemies are constant in the minds of those who read, watch, and remember—images of peasants in feudal Europe who had to yield their brides to rapacious landlords or their crops to the plunderers called knights. They were enemies. Of war's victims any time, any place, for some of whom the enemy was a remote plotter over maps and charts whereas for others the enemy was the lustful killer who invaded the home, gorged on the last stores of food, attacked the women, and set fire to the cottage. Other images: of those who suffered in bad marriages, wherein the one who should share the bed shows demonic ingenuity in depriving the other of dignity. Of honest politicians defeated by the Big Lie. Of victims of Big Lie politicians who, in power, move against the innocent. Of employees destroyed by less than innocent competition, made unemployed by caprice or malign intent. None of them would have trouble identifying with the psalmists.

Wilhelm Dilthey, a great nineteenth-century scholar, once wrote that as a modern, he had difficulty identifying with many kinds of past experiences. One example unlocks a problem for any who today deal with the psalms. Dilthey used the illustration of Martin Luther's sense of terror and sorrow before God. A modern person cannot easily imagine making a bed into a "river of tears." Guilt in the face of divine anger does not come that easily to a healthy-minded and busy contemporary. Today, a guilty person reflects that guilt back against parents who make demands we cannot meet, spouses who casually deny affection, or nameless and faceless forces that never take the name or shape of God. Yet, Dilthey said, even these other reflections make possible some sympathy with people like the psalmists and Luther. A thoughtful person can have analogous experiences. Through imagination he can feel empathy with people of the past whose every move was dominated by real, not imagined, enemies.

Karl Rahner may have unwittingly limited the scope for those who have a wintry sort of spirituality when he asked for *intellectual* solidarity with those who are of alien outlooks. People have become disillusioned, doubting, and despairing not simply because they have gone through the experience of modern rationalism. Sometimes they instead have simply had what we might call the modern experience, and therefore have been unable to include God in their horizon.

Many of these people are not as articulate as are the intellectual seekers and rejecters. Some of them are aged citizens who live in ghettos where they are surrounded by young enemies. They have to chart their trips to the market as carefully as generals plan defensive military campaigns. An innocent ride in the elevator can be interrupted by the flash of a knife toward a throat, a reach for a pocketbook, an open door and a darting thief. A walk to the car from a church door becomes a nightmare. There is always the specter of a hand reaching around a mouth.

The enemy of such a helpless aged person can also be the merchant who prices the food at a supermarket. Others are the corrupt magistrates who allow permits for taverns where

noise and danger threaten seniors because these establish-
ments serve as centers for narcotic sales in quiet neighbor-
hoods. The enemy can be the judge who dispenses injustice,
or the welfare worker who demeans the one who needs
service. Not to see the world through the eyes of the victims
is to be cut off from humanity. Refusing to hear or tell the
story of suffering is brutalizing. To be ready for the story is
to be positioned in front of the psalms.

One last demurrer is in order before the modern winterer
falls into step next to the victims of enemies. Merely because
the psalms may be conceived of as divinely inspired or as a
supreme form of spiritual literature need not mean that they
should have such a privileged place that all their lines fall
beyond the range of criticism. There are many expressions
and experiences in sacred scriptures that one would not set
out to emulate. These ancient writings come from many
angles of vision. They tell of fools and sinners, false starters
and evil completers. No humane person would counsel a
father today to listen to the voice of a divine messenger or
deity if it commanded sacrifice of a son. Yet the story of
Abraham and Isaac honors such a command. No believer in
the God of the Bible would congratulate a Jephthah who
kept his vow to sacrifice the first person he met after a
victory—only to confront his own daughter. There may also
be good reasons not to follow the psalmists at all points.
Often there are no civil ways for one to share one's impulse.
Who could wish that the children of enemies be dashed
against a wall?

THE MANY ROLES ENEMIES PLAY

Emboldened by such thoughts that free us from the texts,
we can venture to question the role of the enemy in so many
psalms. This lyrical literature, one surmises, would have
gained in both poetic power and psychological depth had

the writers been able to take control of themselves and keep their enemies off at some psychological distance. Most obsession with enemies sounds like scapegoating. The dialogue with the self goes like this: "If I cannot solve something in my life, I turn to fault outside forces. The enemy is easily blamable. If the foe were not there to trip me up, my future would be clear. Were he not there to tempt or threaten me, then I could think thoughts that would bring me close to God." The enemy, in all these turns of thought, is a convenient character whom I can bring on stage to manipulate and deflect me from self-analysis or from taking blame.

An opposing set of thoughts also crowds into the mind. These psalms live because they *do* address permanent and profound human needs. Sheltered and protected persons need texts to help them find imagination to identify with people whose lives are dominated by an enemy. Such imagination helps prepare them for a moment when their secure and complacent worlds are shattered in an instant. A home invader, the military draft, a scam or confidence game, a rival in love, a vindictive officer of the law, a competitor in business—any of these may come across a threshold into a settled world and instantly cause it to quake. In the face of such realities, the world in front of the psalmic text is never really remote. Wherever on its spare midwinter landscape the psalmist outlasts the threat of winterkill, he offers a promising way of living.

My notebook based on a reading of the psalms includes more in this "response-to-enemies" category than any other. In many cases the themes are repetitive. The disciplined reader of the texts nevertheless will find in their course a number of major themes supplementing and enhancing each other in support of some major motifs. One can turn the pages almost at random and let these psalms and themes work their varied effects. Here is Psalm 40.

"Misfortunes beyond counting press on me from all sides" (40:12) sounds the note of what we might call hemmed-in-ness. This language includes physical disintegration: "my sight fails." And one hears expression of a sense of personal fault. Then, as often, the psalmist rises to face the threat of the enemy. "Let those who cry 'Hurrah!' at my downfall be horrified at their reward of shame" (40: 15).

These lines cannot belong in the noblest rank of prayers. Vengeance born of rage, and nothing more generous than that, motivates them. We cannot now retrace our steps to the incident behind this text. No one can find out whether actual enemies did say "Hurrah!" or whether the gifted, wounded writer merely put this word into their minds and on their tongues as a way of reading *what* they would say *if* they said anything. Interestingly, this worrying about "hurrahs!" appears after the psalmist has already thanked the Lord for his rescue "out of the mire and the clay," the rescue that inspired this startling song of praise.

FROM BRAVADO TO RAGE

Some anti-enemy psalms include a tone of bravado that, one suspects, could easily disappear in the face of newer, bigger problems. One recent translation reconstructs a text to envision God as a textwriter, a chronicler, and an accountant: "Enter my lament in thy book, store every tear in thy flask" (56:8). This line occurs in the context of one of the almost paranoid depictions of assault by an outsider. The snowscape of winterkill has seldom appeared more vivid: "All day long abuse of me is their only theme, all their thoughts are hostile. In malice they are on the look-out, and watch for me, they dog my footsteps" (56:5–6). In these lines we detect the tone of one who gains security through a too easy relation to God: "But, while they lie in wait for me, it is they who will not escape" (56:7). But, no, there is real confidence here. It results from the fact that the writer has an ally. Since he has put his trust in God, he asks: "What can mortal men do to me?" (56:4). Yet it sounds almost too easy. Other psalms persist in seeing a devastating threat on the part of the enemies. Their author does not foresee early or easy rescue.

Where there is not bravado, there is something apparently even less helpful. Some defenses against the enemy are spoken in an indefensible tone. They might well drive respectable godless moderns into more certified and firm godlessness. Who would have much to do with a God to whom one appeals only after having lost control? He calls God onto the scene to wreak vengeance.

Our children used to dispense fake traffic tickets. They filled these out and placed them under the windshields of autos in parking lots whenever someone hogged two spaces. This ticket, in fine legal print, offered choice maledictions: "May you stall in traffic jams and may the fleas from a thousand camels afflict your armpits." Such tickets stand in a great tradition of malediction. In the Christian Middle Ages, there were people who moved beyond amateur status in such speaking against others. Before one can re-emerge into a zone where psalmists speak with positive spiritual eloquence, it is important to hear them when they, too, sound out of control.

Psalm 109 is one of these poems. It speaks out of and to the rage of angry people who would understandably find my talk of shelter from enemies to be a sign that I had lived life in a protected range of acquaintances and contexts. This psalm, they would say, reflects exactly how things are. At least and at last such psalms talk about the real world. What is the fault of these enemies in Psalm 109? They have "heaped calumnies" and told lies. Who has been protected from their kind? Their attacks, made without cause, are worse because those who spoke them were repaying "hatred in return for my love" (109:2,5).

Then come the maledictions. "May his days be few; may his hoarded wealth fall to another! May his children be fatherless, his wife a widow! May his children be vagabonds and beggars, driven from their homes! May the money-lender distrain on all his goods and strangers seize his earnings! May none remain loyal to him, and none have mercy on his fatherless children! May his line be doomed to extinction, may their name be wiped out within a generation! (109:8–13). The psalmist wants the curse to "seep into his body like water and into his bones like oil!" (109:18).

With a psalmist like that for a friend, one will not likely rise above the emptiness of uncreative rage. Such a psalm inspires ingenuity from pious commentators, none of whom would admire this kind of language among their contemporaries. They try to retranslate the psalm. They place the curses into the mouths of the enemy, but that effort does violence to the texts. Others resort to reminders that here and there the Hebrew Scriptures include lines to the effect that those who show hatred—presumably the enemy, not the psalmist—will have to face a God who can only curse and abandon them.

All these moderating efforts fail in the end. The psalm is there to serve as a scandal. It is a necessary element in the season of winterkill, when white-heated rage against the enemy turns uncreative. To all purposes, it blocks out the very God who is being invoked.

While a cursing rage serves as evident therapy for a psalmist when he has lost self-control, a self-confident righteousness appears in other places. A creatively suspicious analyst of our times would want to ask some questions. How are you sure *you* are innocent? Why is the enemy always wrong and why are you always right?

Psalm 7 is rich in language that places the writer above the enemy, "for I am clearly innocent" (7:8). God can express revenge because of this affected innocence; the Lord has "tipped his arrows with fire" (7:13) to pursue the enemy. Only one note of tentativeness sneaks in with a cautionary "if": "if I have done any of these things—if I have stained my hands with guilt, if I have repaid a friend evil for good," then may the adversary trample me (7:3–5). Whoever identifies with this psalm is protected from pure pride by the knowledge that the author is not claiming to be perfect, only generally just. This more modest claim makes the appeal plausible. Still, this is not the purest form of piety. It merely reflects emotions unreined.

The same tone is present in Psalm 17, where a constant appeal for help sounds because of the poet's innocence. A very gentle image introduces the lament: "Keep me like the apple of thine eye; hide me in the shadow of thy wings" (17:8). "The apple" is the pupil, believed long ago to be the most precious element and thus most valuable to a protector. God is to be as tender as the mother bird who covers the young in the face of storm or predators. Then follows the violent reaction to those "wicked who obstruct," the foes who surround the faithful (17:9).

Modern novelists do well to strain for economy of words like these in order to speak of the sense of being cornered. They would reproduce the reaction of the eloquently terrified animal around whom the hunters are circling toward almost inevitable doom: "They press me hard, now they hem me in, on the watch to bring me to the ground" (17:11). Not only the hunter stalks: "The enemy is like a lion eager for prey, like a young lion crouching in ambush" (17:12). The mood that goes with hunter action and hunted reac-

tion chills the psalm, despite its own warm counteractive imagery. Only a person who feels cornered can easily identify with it. One utters it momentarily en route to a deeper piety, and then must forget it immediately after the utterance: "Thrust them out of this world in the prime of their life, gorged as they are with thy good things" (17:14). This phrase breathes the spirit of envy untempered by the speaker's sense that any engorgement is gross and demeaning, a barrier to spiritual development.

When the reader is ready to turn the page in search of a more valid prayer, her eye suddenly falls on the most quiet kind of plea for a person who is about to sleep. Like many such phrases, it helps one work through and past the inappropriate and misfit pages of the psalms to those that hint at light: "I shall see thy face, and be blest with a vision of thee when I awake" (17:15). Even hemmed-in, cornered, hunted suppliants can get the enemy off their minds enough to let sleep, even disturbed sleep, arrive.

One of the most ambitious of these expressions in the face of enemies is Psalm 35. In a strange way it is more appealing, is more able to attract sympathetic hearers. Here it has become clear that a generally modest, shall we say, bourgeois, type of victim has felt the weight of injustice. He speaks for the many of us who feel we have simply gone about our business, quietly supporting law, order, and decency, only to be misused. "Malicious witnesses step forward" (35:11). "When I slipped, brutes who would mock even a hunchback ground their teeth at me" (35:16). This image is compelling because it has the ring of contemporary reportage. Who would speak this way without having just been in the presence of people who are vicious? They have had to be violent to inspire the hunchback reference, which is not the kind that comes easily to a relaxed mind. Again one hears "Hurrah!" (35:21, 25) when the writer is in misfortune. Taunting upsets him more than torture. The Lord, though, having seen this, has been keeping silence and remains unstirred.

Moderns identify with this. The Catholic worker in a Latin American republic dispenses what measure of justice she can among villagers as she cares for victims in revolution. In the midst of mixed feelings occasioned by violence on all sides, she is clear about her purposes. She sees herself on God's side, if not God on her side, intervening in history. Enemies arise, to threaten and taunt her. The regime, media, backbiters all conspire to misrepresent her. In her mind, they live by the lie and the sarcastic phrases of the powerful. Let her be raped and they will have their "Hurrah!"—what business did a do-gooder have in such a place? She is accused by some of the very people she served who, seeking advantage for themselves, step forward in malice to witness.

Outrage over injustice ranks higher in our minds than does disturbance over our personal discomfort. This awareness begins to ennoble and enlarge the view of the enemy in our minds. It makes possible a more generous spirituality, while still doing justice to the hurt and the rage of cornered people. We learn that such emotions are natural and have their place. In any case, in the world in front of this text God is called upon to join in a battle that has already begun:

"Strive, O Lord, with those who strive against me" (35:1). The hunted one, still outraged over injustice, barters a bit: let rescue come, "so shall I talk of thy justice and of thy praise all the day long" (35:28).

THE BEGINNINGS OF TRUST

No longer need we hold a sulking psalmist at arm's length. Here is the beginning of a trust in God, a trust that still moves the heart. When complacent in an armchair, we can judge the slightly too righteous psalmist. Engagement in struggles for justice, on the other hand, demands a summoning of all emotional and spiritual energies. The source of these is the mysterious trust that offers what warmth one can expect to feel in the season of winterkill.

Ours presently is a course of spiritual pursuit that makes no pretense that we can simply meditate or contemplate ourselves into range of the deity. We have spoken of our quest as a kind of hitchhiking on the moral experience of others. We are, in positive ways, parasites on the verbal expression of those who have left us with timeless texts. Such a focus draws us into a sphere where words matter very much. A person cannot fail to notice how in these psalms that are directed against enemies the victim complains against the damage that potent words can effect. Gossip, slander, backbiting, talebearing, lying, false witness—all these seem to be greater threats than are physical ones. To the degree that this is so, the psalmist thereby pays a compliment to the power of words. Psalm 12 picks up this motif.

"Loyalty is no more; good faith between man and man is over" (12:1). The writer knows how the I and Thou break apart into iciness when, behind words, the trust is gone. "One man lies to another: they talk with smooth lip and double heart," saying "words are our ally; who can master us?" (12:2,4). As so often elsewhere, the author puts himself in a circle from which all others seem to be alienated. The prophets of Israel on numbers of occasions spoke from this vantage: no one else is left to speak the truth, to be loyal, say people like Elijah. For speaking the truth, their own lives are in danger. In this psalm, the author is wise enough to see what it is that such claims for the power of words can do: "Who can master us?" is a prideful question as old as Eden. It places the person in the rank of God.

THE SAVING POWER IN WORDS

The writer shows how he treasures words when he contrasts those of his enemies with God's. "The words of the Lord are pure words: silver refined in a crucible, gold seven times purified" (12:6). However one conceives of hearing those words—for most of us they are reflected in scriptures like these—their value is clear. In the face of lying and hypocrisy, they serve as a measure of the distance God keeps from the deceptive human world. "Pure words" have the further effect of quickening thoughtful people not to measure their spiritual life by the language of their enemies or even flattering friends. Only one source has pure words to provide a standard for all others.

Other psalms witness to the effect of words. In Psalm 59 there is evidence that enemies know they need an audience. If there is no one to hear, what is the point of speaking? Here, as so often, the enemies prowl and howl (59:6, 15); "From their mouths comes a stream of nonsense; 'But who will hear?' they murmur" (59:7).

This kind of taunt is frequent in the Hebrew Scriptures. Let psalmists and others of the faithful cry out; but where *is* God? Who will answer the cry? Here again is the wintry cry of Absence, Absence. Immediately God must be vindicated: "But thou, O Lord, dost laugh at them, and deride all the nations" (59:8). A divine sneer clears the field of all enemies. "But I will sing of thy strength, and celebrate thy love when morning comes" (59:16). Here is no proof for the existence of God, no reasoning that there are divine ears to hear. Instead there remains only the witness of a heart. In the face of the enemies, it finds reasons to abide close in loyalty to a voice that has spoken and beckoned for trust before.

The notion of the divine laugher echoes also when the poet joins, not always in an admirable, but often with an understandable, spirit. In Psalm 54, God is to vindicate the writer against insolent and ruthless people. At the end, the task is accomplished: "God has rescued me from every trouble, and I look on my enemies' downfall with delight" (54:7). This phrase, some say, is not sounded in the spirit of triumphal gloating. Rather it expresses mere delight in faith's victory. Such an explanation sounds a bit too glossy. Must every misfit psalm be tailored to fit more civil sensibilities? The enmity of others, let it be stated and faced again, lest its presence inspire mere guilt, can be so strong that the most natural compensatory attitude is to clap hands when the enemy meets disaster.

THE BIRTH OF TRUST

The last word of this set of psalms does not find satisfaction in the triumph of enemies but of God. It does not celebrate the victory of lying but of pure words and truth, not devastations by disloyalty but the confidence of trust. This expression, dire though it may be, is not a signal of mere winter but of a wintry sort of spirituality. Even on the chill terrain where the enemies circle and close in, a sign of affirmation appears.

Curiously, the attacks by enemies inspire strong Yeses. When psalm writers are left alone, to concentrate on the natural limits of their lives, the Yes is less forthcoming. Anger them and they will seek alliance. This theme finds its echo in much of the history of spirituality. The active saint is never left to her own resources. Beleaguered, set upon, persecuted she may be, but all the attacks "get her dander up." She feels a new hunger for divine presence. According to the autobiographies of saints, this hunger then becomes most palpable. The remoteness of God is a problem for the psalmist when faceless fears from within attack. On the other hand, God is near for the defense of the attacked, especially when vivid enemies impinge.

Psalm 55 speaks to the contrast. "I am panic-stricken at the shouts of my enemies" (55:3). "My heart is torn with anguish and the terrors of death come upon me. Fear and trembling overwhelm me and I shudder from head to foot" (55:4–5). With this outcry comes a more calm report about the surrounding world. "I have seen violence and strife in the city . . . its public square is never free from violence and spite" (55:9, 11). This time, however, there is also a surprise, the deepest cut of all. This time no enemy does the taunting. The poet turns suddenly and startles the bystander with pointed finger and searching scowl: "It was you, a man of my own sort, my comrade, my own dear friend, with whom I kept pleasant company in the house of God" (55:13–15). Wounded, hurt, enraged, the writer piles on likenesses of the word friend, friend, friend, all in the language of betrayal. This curse is appropriately weighted, even if it is not appropriate for the kind of behavior: "May death strike them" (55:14), "may they go down alive into Sheol; for their homes are haunts of evil!" (55:15).

The worst need for vengeance comes when the dearest friend is the betrayer. After this point sinks in, the reader needs one of the more serene follow-ups in all the texts. "But I will call upon God; the Lord will save me" (55:16). "He has heard my cry" (55:18). God "gave me back my peace" (55:18). This time the psalmist turns didactic, singling out the reader: "Commit your fortunes to the Lord, and he will sustain you; he will never let the righteous be shaken" (55:22).

That a wintry sort of spirituality survives these rages of winterkill is clear from Psalm 3. This short poem generalizes about the many enemies, who keep multiplying to say "God will not bring him victory" (3:2). In the midst of these taunts, the psalmist displays serenity. In quiet defiance he turns his back to the enemies, his body to the wall, and his face to the Lord. "I lie down and sleep, and I wake again, for the Lord upholds me" (3:5). Abruptly one can envision a theology in defense of sleep, which is a gift signaling so much confidence that the reader need no longer keep an eye open for the enemy. No corner of his mind is to be distracted by the need to keep the foe at a distance.

The texts offer few strategies to use against the enemy beyond complaining, calling out for God, laughing back, and demonstrating that one can sleep. One tactic, employed both as an instrument and for its own sake, is useful to anyone who now wants to keep at a distance the enemies of spiritual life. The psalms are documents of personal faith, but they are set in the context of a community. For the author, this community found its central focus in the house of the Lord. In Psalm 27, after sounding the standard complaint against enemies, he pens a quiet announcement about how to be sustained: "that I may be constant in the house of the Lord all the days of my life, to gaze upon the beauty of the Lord and to seek him in his temple" (27:4). Reference to a familial warmth follows: "Though my father and my mother forsake me, the Lord will take me into his care" (27:10). "Well

99

I know that I shall see the goodness of the Lord in the land of the living" (27:13).

Psalm 27 ends with counsel that shows the author rising above the challenge of enemies. It includes a tactic that has always been demanded of spiritually serious people. In the face of the drama between good and evil, self versus friends and enemies, the psalmist advises: "Wait for the Lord; be strong, take courage, and wait for the Lord" (27:14). The forces that would kill on the stormy landscape of the frightened heart do not, after all, have the last word.

The psalm reflects other counsel from within the Hebrew Scriptures. Much of it is of the sort that has long sustained people who work in causes for justice. Black slaves whose bids for freedom were so long thwarted, revolutionaries who were put down by regimes, dreamers who were boxed in by realists, have often turned to this resource. One text that has often haunted and enlivened people in struggles is Habakkuk 2:3: "For there is still a vision for the appointed time. At the destined hour it will come in breathless haste, it will not fail. If it delays, wait for it; for when it comes will be no time to linger." We have by now come far from the company of a psalmist who found nothing at first to do but to want to see the children of enemies killed. In this stage now, he invites readiness to wait for the Lord.

6. January Thaw: A Hint of Presence

THE WINTERBOURNE FLOW IN THE HEART

While silence, chill, and threat of death overall mark the wintry climate and landscape, exceptions are evident. Suddenly a figurative rivulet flows from under the ice. In parts of England where chalk deposits are present, people call such streams "winterbourne." They flow in the season when nothing else is liquid. Small freshets, they would be lost among the spring torrents or the summer rush of rivers. But on a morning when nothing else in nature stirs to violate the motionless still, the alert ear can hear winterbourne ripple.

The silence and the chill of the heart also know such interruptions. The winterers cannot yet look for long days or the warmth of spring. The slant of the hemisphere is too far from the sun to permit such a prospect. For reasons not easy to discern or explain, the heart also slants from the warmth of affirmation, the glow of a benign universe, the heat of the divine presence. Yet the seasons in the heart, just as the season in nature, allow for exceptions to the chill. The old almanacs liked to talk about "January thaw," a moment that has its parallel in the experience of believers' souls.

The wintry sort of spirituality, let it be remembered, stakes out its place on the landscape next to persons who have seen God excluded from their horizons. That exclusion is the signal of their wintriness. They have not given up on the search for God. They remain committed to the Christian meanings, and they find many occasions to worship and affirm. That is the sign of their spirituality. They may be most hungry for the sound of winterbourne rippling or eager for the slight increase in temperature that allows them to open a jacket they had closed against the wind. They would pause on the journey to look up for a moment at a cloudless sky. They cannot satisfy their hunger by reading the descriptions of summery piety. They have to find their Yes on the colder, more barren landscape.

January thaw: those who must endure the worst of winter have mixed feelings about this moment. They do not dare to settle in to it with security. They fear its deceptive character. In this sense the time is something like Indian summer, which also deceives. For an instant it promises to bring back summer after the first frost. For a moment those who enjoy it are tempted to delude themselves: "The climate in which we live has changed." The thermometers suggest to residents of the northlands that they might begin to partake of the warmth in which southerners always bask. This year, maybe, the weather will not be so bad! Yet while the pores open to warmth, the head knows what the dates on the calendar insist upon. Indian summer will soon slip away, yielding to the winter freeze and the long cold season ahead.

In a similar sense January thaw also lulls. If Indian summer brought back remembrance of the season past, January thaw anticipates the warmer one to come. Even far from the chalky winterbourne landscape, a few streams flow again. The earlier ice that came after solstice begins to thin. A branch falls on it and it breaks. A puddle from the stream forms upon the crystal ice and seems to take courage from its own ripples. Such motion breaks more ice, until a track of running water creates its stream within the stream between the banks of ice. Snow on the roof thins, slides to the eaves, its melt adding at night to the gutter icicles. In the next day's sun it breaks off with the whole icicle and clears from the roof and the gutter. Birds that had been sheltered —where?—emerge in coyness, squint at the kitchen window, flit to the feeder, indulge themselves, and if they do not actually break into song, emit little sounds against the wintry silence.

The human heart knows such moments of fresh flow or eruptions of sound when these were unexpected. Yet the heart that wants to be deluded and lulled is countered, in a whole human being, by a head that *knows*. The spiritual January thaw will not last. Enjoy the warmth and sound it brings, the heart tells itself, but know that this is not a dispelling of winter, only an interruption.

The value of momentary relief

The January thaw and the winterbourne stream do offer relief. The mind that knows the temptations of delusion need not fall to them. Enjoyment of relief is a better use for the momentary warmth. Winter unbroken is more than the heart can sustain. Emotional equivalents to cabin fever are deadening. Only so long can a person be spiritually confined without any pause, any surprise. God is ahead, a seeker is told, God is always ahead, always promising spring. She lives by hope, but is it to be a hope that never finds any sort of ratification? That seems like no hope at all. Why must God belong always and only to the future? When I move ahead in time will God always and only remain future? Waiting for God is creative, but has God never a motion or word for this day? In this wintry moment when I need God most, what point is there to mere waiting and hoping?

The relief January thaw brings comes in the form of promise. One corner of the heart and mind remains on guard, alert to the knowledge that this brighter moment will pass. From another corner come the questions: Is this relief, is this brighter? Or is it something cruel, like the narrow shaft of sun that breaks on the floor of a dungeon whose gate will never open, a prison whose bars will never yield? Is this experience comparable to the walk a condemned person gets to take in the sun of the prison yard the day before execution? If there is food for the spirit, is it thrown as casually as that tossed to the backyard bird—and thus to be seen as the subject of caprice, to be forgotten and absent tomorrow?

The heart has many sides, however, and still other sides bring different messages. January thaw will not last. Tomorrow the weather may chill again. Rather than ask questions of waiting and hoping, rather than live always and only toward tomorrow, should I not also see intrinsic value in today? The intrinsicalness of moments, especially times of relief, merits celebration during any spiritual pilgrimage. A person does not bring comfort to the terminally ill in order to win their friendship for a reciprocal turn some future year. There may not be a future year for reciprocity. Instead, the patient only makes demands, and there is to be only a gesture that the other can never return. Yet that gesture of comfort and care represents the whole world on this day, both for the recipient who values it on its own terms and for the one who extends it. In extending comfort, he recognizes again the value of a bonding gesture and asks nothing about tomorrow.

When on a bed of pain, a patient welcomes the hours without pain even if there will be future hours with new pain. Even temporary painlessness is good on its own terms. In various ways all people are on a terminal course. Cells in the body move toward their inevitable end. Yet while they threaten resistlessly the death of the body, the people in whom they work read poetry, welcome psalms, make love, enjoy the cup and the table, and bask in friendship. In every case such affirmers celebrate the intrinsic value of the gifts or the acts without reference to past or future. Through these acts of valuing, they became more able to live without guilt about the past and fear for the future.

Humankind cannot bear too much reality, wrote T. S. Eliot. A person cannot stare too long at the sun or at death, said La Rochefoucauld. To this duo we can add, "nor at winter." To have something else than mere reality to bear for a moment or a season need not be delusion. To be free to look at winterbourne instead of only at icy streams, at the drip of water on the end of an icicle instead of only at the glacial freeze: these can be sustaining acts that equip a person for many futures. The heart has its rhythms that the mind does not always know. The mind, as it comes to know somehow, can feed the heart.

The relief that spells a wintry sort of spirituality does not necessarily evolve into summery sorts. It seeks styles appropriate for its own character and season. Those who follow the disciplines of this character by letting the psalms work their effects will find a peculiar focus on every few pages of psalm texts. Relief in the form of January thaw comes when the meditator upon those pages assumes a certain responsibility for the seasonal bleakness. The world in front of the psalms texts perpetuates the mystery of God-caused starkness. Never does it suggest that those who do well will live forever on earth or know nothing but prosperity. That world insists instead that beginnings and ends are in the hands of God. Nor is the universe of nature excused: death is a natural act, as one generation makes space for the next. Nothing I do, says the reader who hitchhikes on the experience of psalmists, *nothing I do* can rearrange the universe and make me God or give me power over nature. There *are*, however, things I can do to help dispel delusion and find a measured relief in the midst of winter, in my spiritual January thaw.

THE DISCOVERY OF SPIRITUAL RESPONSIBILITY

Psalms that concentrate on moral failure, including seven often called penitential, allow for the reflective believer to take some responsibility for the temperature and climate in the face of God and the universe. They speak boldly and frankly about evil in the mind and heart. These prayers picture that the God who cares at all also cares about deviation from the proper path. The universe itself appears to fall out of line because the sinner is misaligned with respect to the purposes of God. The misalignment produces a creative terror, one that can lead to a changed direction.

Awareness of the disparity between what is and what should be in the world that lies in front of the psalms text can lead to a variety of responses. In the sin-sick soul, it leads to a vital sense of the threatening presence of God. The nearness, not the distance, of God becomes the problem, not because of divine inscrutability, but because the divine wrath appears now to be so palpable and ominous. The sinner comes in fear and sorrow to the presence of this God, who then shows another face, a gracious mien. What follows is eternal summer in the heart. So the scriptural texts often and elsewhere say. Under what impulse would anyone remain cautious during this onrush of grace into the summery heart? Those who nurture a wintry sort of spirituality often seem defeated by the very signals that cheer others. If the summery types are to claim a monopoly for their experience of God, then the wintry sorts can have no experience at all. No psychological technique permits them to match in any clear detail what their enthusiastic counterparts profess to own. If anything, the testimony of the easily warmed heart alienates the seeker. Describe a work of art to the blind, signal the meaning of music to the deaf, and you may promote as much frustration as enjoyment.

Will the Yes become theirs as they share the world that opens in front of the psalm texts? If these texts are to disclose other ways of being in the world, at first glance it would seem that the only ways shown begin with God at the center of the landscape. God is the terror and the promise. Wilhelm Dilthey's question reappears. What shall I do when I read of religious experiences like those of the psalmist or of Martin Luther and find no easy way to connect with them? Try as I might, I can not "make a river of my bed with tears." Whereas others asked, "Is God gracious?" I ask, "Is God?"; does God appear at all? My heaven is not too threatening with the nearness of God. Instead it seems empty and silent. My horizon knows no skyline of the City of God. It only offers more distant horizons. Dilthey, be it remembered, advised that moderns must seek analogous experiences. They should trade on the similarities-within-differences that make possible some empathy for the world of the psalms.

The spiritual project of the theologian Paul Tillich was directed to this theme. Where the ancient felt sin-sick, he said as he spoke for many, I feel only the absence of meaning. Where the psalmist felt threatened, I feel alienated. Where Luther felt impinged upon by a too-near God, I feel abandoned by a too-remote God. The "I" can, however, be quickened to many kinds of experiences. Responsiveness to the biblical texts is a first venture toward such quickening and opening. I can not readily find the other modes of being readily disclosed. Patience makes its demands. Finding the Yes will not, for the wintry sort, be a turn to the simple "Aha!" that more buoyant people experience. Yet the Yes does not withhold its promise entirely for those who read, who open, who imagine.

CALLING IT GUILT, SPEAKING OF SIN

Have we here hurried too fast past the possibility that modern people might also experience sin-sickness? Guilt of nameless, faceless, ill-focused sorts has never fallen into short supply. People in whole industries, equipped with couches and staffed by people with medical credentials, minister to those who feel guilt. Some of these who feel guilt are religious and godly, while others are not religious and recognize no presence of God. The effects in both cases are similar. They both live lives haunted by yesterday, under the lengthened shadows of parents whose demands they never met or could meet. These victims are torn apart by memories of words snapped cruelly at spouses, promises too easily made in love and too readily broken in hatred. They suffer from addictions that have enslaved them and kept them unfree in the face of bids for attention from others.

In the world revealed in the psalms, guilt is related to sin; but in recent times the connection has seemed to be broken. *Whatever Became of Sin?* asked the psychiatrist Dr. Karl Menninger at a cultural moment when guilt raged and sin, he thought, went unmentioned. His book on that subject was itself a contribution to the recovery of the sin-sense and thus a warming sign on the wintry spiritual landscape. Call something sin, recognize it as such, and you verge toward affirmation. Sin is appropriate as a term only when the horizon is not permanently voided of God. Sin relates to the language of *I* and *Thou.* I sin *against* Thee. I break a relation. "Nothing personal," says the modern about guilt. "Something personal," says the spiritual winterer who must connect guilt and sin.

Whatever became of sin? It came back, it has been coming back, throughout this century of the second Christian millennium. Early moderns shied away from the concept as being too demeaning. They offered other explanations for the temporary setbacks humans knew in their relentless upward march. Yes, said the American Christian modernist Lyman Abbott, surely, the human race stumbles momentarily in its inevitable upward climb. Then it stops to bandage its knee, picks itself up, resumes walking, and again takes up the climb. He was talking—can we believe this?—about the world of World War I. Abbott was overlooking the errancy and hatred that produced trench warfare and battles on the hellscape of Verdun and the Marne. Let 600,000 casualties appear within a week in such a battle, and let Europe's young men fall into the sloughs of utter futility. The progressivist, overlooking sin and minimizing guilt, could put on blinders and never search the heart. He could only perpetuate faith in the inevitable upward climb.

Sin came back, some said, when titanic scholars with names like Barth and Niebuhr explored the world in front of the texts of the Epistle to the Romans, the Book of Psalms, and the works of Saint Augustine. They found no more appropriate explanation of humanly caused disaster than concepts that Christians had long before coded under the term Original Sin. Reinhold Niebuhr near the end of his life admitted that he had made a mistake in pedagogy when he tried to resuscitate the category Original Sin. He *had* intended to shock, but instead of scandalizing the way the message of God should, it provoked amusement or confusion because it sounded archaic. Some people Niebuhr wanted to stir smiled at the quaintness and dismissed it. Others shrugged. Original Sin belonged to fate, so it deprived humans of responsibility.

Was it a pedagogical mistake? Perhaps, but Niebuhr did not back away from the bluntness of the reality to which the antique term pointed. If anything, its museumlike character and its long repose in the corners of theological dictionaries worked against its being able to devastate with explanatory power. The biblical and early Christian worlds out of which it emerged seemed domesticated compared to the violent scenes the modern mind and heart could create. Verdun and the Marne, but not they alone, marked the century. One cannot take up pen to write "Buchenwald" or "Auschwitz" without knowing that the names can reduce to cliché the hundred million gasps of pain and cries of bewilderment in the death camps. They do serve, however, as code names in the new era. To invoke them and the sum of Nazi, Soviet, and Maoist death camp horrors is to convoke powers that seem to come from a nether earth. One hears the demonic wingbeat ever closer. It rises from the earth, soars over the desert landscape of the century, threatens, waits for the kill, kills, devours the carrion, leaves a spare carcass, and rests, only soon to fly again.

Whatever became of sin? From the more secure world of white-collared burghers, sin was swept away. In its place came notions like "executive crime," "fudged tax returns," "ripping off" the boss's paper clips. Whatever became of sin? It was routinized in the form of anger that engulfed the human generations and broadened the gulf between them. Offspring and parents for selfish reasons found no warrants to understand or love each other. Spouses made no room for each other on their separating paths toward self-fulfillment.

Media leaders learned new ways to manipulate and deceive. Warmongers found beguiling words to make the seekers of peace sound naive and foolish. Sin came back, renamed.

Why should sin turn up in texts whose positive thrust is to give readers experiences that are the emotional equivalent of January thaw? The term sin seems to be a brutal intrusion. It chills, like the crustlet of ice that forms at night over the winterstream to remind the observer that spring is nowhere in prospect. The world in front of the psalmic text, however, makes clear that awareness of sin can bring an arousal of passion and imagination. Sin? Sin against? Sin against whom? Against a silent universe at the edge of an emptied horizon? Sin *only* against the spouse or the neighbor, or when there is mistreatment of soul and body, against the self? On the horizon alongside those who have excluded the presence of God, the questioning half-believer finds that such questions poise the possibility that God will be disclosed as both a threatening and a promising presence.

Psalms that address this presence are not passive. They do not allow for passivity. They set out to give expression for those who have already begun to stir, or they inspire the first commotions. The passive reader becomes active; the victim of impersonal forces becomes an agent among personal ones. On a first reading, these psalms may not achieve all their purposes among moderns. It would be a denial of our wintry sort of search to promise that they will ever do so fully. Because of their usage of beckoning, however, they reveal the promise and motivate more of the search. In that prospect, the reader who opens these psalms allows for a creative jostling of his world. A thousand times his eye may previously have scanned these texts. His ear has often filtered those that appear in liturgies. His mind has dozed as their familiar cadences rolled. A thousand and first time—oh, wonder!—his soul may become attentive, and he may hear with freshness.

THE VALUE OF THE LANGUAGE OF A CRY

Winter thaw in the landscapes of the heart begins with the language of a cry. Such a cry is itself affirming because it focuses on a direction. This is not a mere cry into the night against a starless heaven under whose silent canopy the church bells ring without ever evoking a response. This shout affirms because it is not merely a crying *out* but a crying *toward.* Psalm 25 voices this type of prayer. The reader recognizes that its passion has been channeled and stylized. This is an acrostic psalm whose verses begin with a sequence of letters in the Hebrew alphabet. Picture the children's ABC books, in which each page must begin with the next letter in the alphabet. Psalm 25 is a bit corrupted and irregular; some letters are missing. But the Hebrew could come to what are today verses 16–21 and hurry through *pē, sādē, rēsh, shīn,* and *tāw.* This could permit a rattling through the *p, r, s,* and *t* zone of the alphabet. On second reading, however, the style works its poetic effect. For a comparison: the sonnet form in English poetry need not mean a reduction of artistic passion. It can help the reader focus through its art. Psalm 25 has a focus because of its cry.

"Turn to me and show me thy favour, for I am lonely and oppressed" (25:16). Aloneness and alienation are not modern inventions, but modern people may find it less easy than did their ancestors to picture the divine face hidden because it is turned. Instead, now friends have closed their doors and shuttered their hearts. They go about their business, one mourns, as if *my* being did not matter. They may picture me accompanied, but they have no imagination for my sense of abandonment when my apartment door closes, the candle burns low, the faucet drip tortures. The divine turning in the psalm is pictured as the first sign of having company. To speak in the outcry we call prayer, to ask for this turning, is to address the Thou, to assume the possibility of the Thou.

"Thou" gets called in, not unexpectedly for anyone familiar with the psalmist's habit of blaming others, to "look at my enemies," to see "how violent their hatred for me" is (25:19). Such fingerpointing in no way advances the case for self-examination. Before it, however, is a better verse that does: "Look at my misery and my trouble and forgive me every sin" (25:18). No one escapes the accusing finger now as it points to the mirror of the reflective heart. Not God, not the silent universe, not the abandoning friend or the taunting enemy serve to explain my plight, at least not any longer; "I" move centerstage in the face of "Thou." I deserve what is happening to me. I am not content to remain in that sad circumstance. This psalm begins the gathering of energies that will in its course call forth passion, quickening, agency.

Such a text as this prematurely domesticates the passions that we are to associate with sin. Cut sin down to size and it figuratively fits in teacups and can be controlled with the temperature of the tea, read with the leaves, warmed with a tiny flame, dispensed with by a toss into the sink.

We need a different note. Certainly there were behind the curtains of France mothers of young dead soldiers, mothers who stared out at tree stumps where forests had been, at ruins where cathedrals had defied the skyline and thought, "I am not responsible." They had nurtured their sons. One day they did what a good parent does, they built up their children's egos and encouraged their promise. On another day, the parents just as carefully cut their offspring down to size, helped them fit into a world. They prayed, paid taxes, followed the commandments, and hated no Germans. Now they are alone and find no consoling friends. "Turn," they bid the "Thou." God turns, and they gain personal peace. As for the enormousness of crimes that lived on in their nation and its enemies?—that was unaddressed.

Across a river and a hundred trenches away, on the second floor of a building in a business district of an untouched, intact German town, a business man might also pace and stare. He had been to mass that morning. Knees bent, he, truly humble, addressed the "Thou." He felt the turning. The man knew his catechism, loved his wife, had a French cousin, and had never hated the English. Why should he be seen as an instrument of hate, a participant in futility and crime? He prayed always and only that the killing would stop, that peace would come, that he and his but not *only* he and his could be secure again. Yet his nation was an agent of the killing, the letting loose of violence on Europe in its First World War. What language might he summon that could do justice to the larger forces of evil?

The wintry sort of spirituality breeds awareness that not everything changes simply because I change. I may personally experience divine turning. It may mean much, may even seem to mean all to me. In the nursing home, who asks for other gifts than this turning by God? In the cancer ward, to know the face of this Presence is to have a reason to relish a word like "benign" against the malignancies that advance. The sin-sick soul, feeling alone in guilt, receives a gift thanks to the turning, but that is never enough.

After the world wars, Christians reread the old texts and found connections in them between "I" and "We" as well as between "I" and "Thou." They began to use words like "collective guilt," "corporate sin," "plural misdeed," and linked these all to the pride of nations. They did so not merely after reading the blood-dripped pages of the twentieth-century Book of the Dead. They came to deep understandings not by reading the statistics of war or by studying the rationales for military action, along with the social scientists' explanations; they needed a bigger fulcrum to move the world's heart. The new readers had to find a stronger

114

lever to lift up the mind. They found it in the experience of the sacred, in what they regarded as the divine transcendence. Their experience and language were shaped on that devastated landscape next to those whose horizons excluded God. They passed these on to the generations that followed.

THE PLACE OF A LAUGHING GOD

Numbers of the chastened modern respondents to these texts opened Psalm 2, there to listen: "Why are the nations in turmoil? Why do the peoples hatch their futile plots?" (2:1). Taken in context, these lines might breed arrogance. We presume that the Judaean kings recited them to stake out their place among the other powers. They are lines that nevertheless fit into a larger canonical context. Then and thus they serve as judgments on Davidic as well as French, German, and American leaders alike. The Why? of these two lines speaks not for the anguish born of abandonment, a language familiar in the most wintry psalms. Instead, this is an active, affirmative, almost defiant "Why?". The psalmist does not understand how nations could act against both God and the people of Israel. The foreign conspiracies just do not know the power against which they rage or the futility of their own armament and plotting.

The world in front of this text comes to its proper perspective when the psalmist sets *all* the nations in the context of transcendence. Now comes a surprising note, a rare biblical air-clearing one: we hear divine laughter. "The Lord who sits enthroned in heaven laughs" to scorn nations and rulers (2:4); We have waited so long for such a laugh. The Lord sits "enthroned in heaven." Here the mind reaches, as minds must, for a spatial and dimensional metaphor. Put the Lord up high so there can be better divine looking down with perspective, more reason for awe among the scurrying and

115

conniving nations whose ways are being shattered. God laughs them to scorn, not in order to scorn for scorning's sake, but to reduce their insolent power.

Laughing to scorn works its effect only if the laugher has credentials and power. The innocent victim who stands on the scaffold below the gallows noose can laugh in his own kind of defiance and disdain. He remains, however, below that noose, and the executioners will certainly take his life. The Lord of history instead laughs to scorn from a position of power over against the minuscule powers whose leaders missed and overestimated their place in history.

Somewhere the poet W. H. Auden made a distinction between the role of the comic and that of the satirist. The comic laughs in order to cope with a world that he cannot change. His is a coming to terms with a misfit universe that otherwise would take the victim wholly captive. The satirist laughs to scorn, almost with a spirit of hope, in order to change a world. The assumption is that people who can put things into perspective and see their limiting contexts might be less foolish than otherwise. Now God is the laugher. God is the one who has the power and the vantage. God's power is evident in the fact that "he threatens them in his wrath" (2:5). Here is God writ large in the figure of an impatient human, in symbolic language that expresses the reality: someone is in control. It matters what responses the nations make.

This psalm, which credentials the Lord to judge the nations, turns soft at the end. Its purpose has not been to picture God as a petty Middle Eastern tyrant who loves to taunt enemies; the divine laughter and wrath are rich in purpose. Anyone can laugh and bear a permanent grudge. The divine passion, however, comes in the form of an anger that need not last, "For his anger flares up in a moment," but "happy are all who find refuge in him" (2:12). No lesser presence would provide a refuge large enough. The divine flaring up, with its threatening and thawing power, is only one aspect of God. The seeker is not content to rest only with this image. The idea of "refuge," however, connects with the portrait of a God strong enough to care about the pride of nations, conspiracy, and violation of divine order.

The transit from our evocation of the people behind French curtains, the man in the German office, or someone in an American study to a throne in the heavens and a perspective on the nations seems too sudden and drastic. Those who move along this transit with ease might evade what the psalms want to probe, which is the difference a laughing, scorning, angered God can make in personal life. Once it is clear that personal life is not a refuge from the collective and corporate misdeeds of nations, the "I" who is part of the "We" becomes central again.

THE INTIMATE ZONE OF LIFE

The writer of Psalm 1 knows and addresses the distinctions between good and evil in that more intimate zone of life. This time the context is not armies and nations but the much smaller circle of friends, the company one keeps. If the arrangement of all the psalms seems to be haphazard, creating the impression of an anthology without plot or scheme, in this one case at least there seems to be plan. Psalm 1 may very well have been placed first to introduce all the psalms. Like so many others, it divides the world in two. In Karl Rahner's terms, such a text seems to position itself where there is a difference between intellectual godliness and godlessness on a parted horizon. Instead, in the psalms, godlessness is usually seen as posing a *moral* choice. Even the godless

117

in these cases *know* there are order, purpose, law, guidance, and God in the universe of meaning. Though aware of it, they choose to ignore the knowledge.

The wintry sort of spirituality calls for an intellectual, but never a moral, solidarity with the godless, with those for whom the very reality of the Lord of Israel has become a problem. The wicked are now "like chaff driven by the wind" (1:4). In our climatic metaphor, they are like dry snow that forms no stable landscape and that will disappear with the thaw. Chaff has no worth. The eye ignores it until and unless the wind stirs it. Chaff or dry snow will have no value and will make no impress on the mind after the wind has blown it away. What humans achieve acquires value when they work against the background of divine agency, which produces something of permanent merit.

All this language is pleasant enough, but still suspicion grows. The introduction to the psalms prepares a reader for the domestic world behind the French curtains, the ordered vantage of the burgher far away from the wars and storms. The psalm texts demand far more than "happiness" and the choice to be positioned with the right company. Yet before we bear down on the texts that leave no escape into the anonymity of the "nation" or "company," it is valuable to have a last passing glance at the "godless" of these psalms.

THE PLACE OF THE HUMAN FOOL

Psalm 14 (and a parallel Psalm 53) addresses the moral ignorance most clearly. A certain character, the fool, comes on stage and then moves off as quickly both times. He becomes irrelevant to the whole plot of the psalms. The act of taking him off stage does call forth some explanation, however. In our time the godless person is often despised by the faithful because of his or her inability to direct intellectual assent or trusting faith toward the God who is the threatening and promising presence in the psalms. Sometimes this godless one is despised as a secular humanist conspirator, someone who willfully resists the call of God and tries to work out satanic purposes.

Karl Rahner, however, has recognized that the Christian with a wintry sort of spirituality begins the search at a base next to precisely such people. For these godless persons reason, science, or literary expression have voided the landscape and emptied the horizons of gods and God. Rahner invited believers to intellectual solidarity with such moderns. He dismissed as invalid what this kind of godless person can do little about. Modern godlessness, while not wholly original, is new enough that it creates new problems and evokes questions that are not fully anticipated in Psalms 14 and 53 or anywhere else in the entire biblical canon.

The late Father John Courtney Murray even used a tinge of ironic expression to locate the modern whose horizon intellectually excludes God. He said such a person violates classic definitions of what it was to be human. Citing Saint John Chrysostom, Murray reminded his contemporaries that in biblical times and through most of the Christian centuries, what we might call godwardness, or god-awareness, belonged to the constitution of the human. To be human was to fear God. Yet, Murray said, whoever has eyes now can look around and find apparently "human" beings who do not fear or know God. Such people are not to exist, but they *do* exist. That is the problem. The problem they raise, because it resonates the way a certain kind of Christian spirituality resonates and because it follows the same rhythm, calls forth a special kind of search and devotion. We can keep *that* kind of godless person on stage. Indeed, we must, if there is to be someone with whom to be empathic.

That is why the different kind of godless fool, the character in Psalms 14 and 53, has to make a quick exit.

"The impious fool says in his heart, 'There is no God.' How vile men are, how depraved and loathsome; not one does anything good!" (14:1). This not too cheerful opener does not point to intellectual atheists, scientific agnostics, or rational humanists. It is not in the mind but in the heart that the word issues: "There is no God." This person arranges life in such a way that the God who does exist and act, the God who is near, is pictured as being ignorable and dismissible. Why? In order that the "vile" fool can live life without responsibility. His world would be the same whether or not he acknowledged God.

THE CRY FROM THE DEPTHS AS AFFIRMATION

No nations, no company of friends, no distractions of the godless occupy the surviving scene on stage. In the penitential psalms everything comes down finally to the moral response of the "I." Sometimes only a solitary cry erupts: "Out of the depths have I called to thee, O Lord; Lord, hear my cry" (130:1). "If thou, Lord, shouldst keep account of sins, who, O Lord, could hold up his head?" (130:3). Even the cry from the depths is an affirmation: Why cry if there is no hint or hope of hearing? Why not mutter to one's self, or sulk? The cry comes with no clear expectations, but it does imply a "Thou." The depths that echo may be glacial crevasses or miring pits. It all does happen this side of Sheol, for the psalms make clear that cries from Sheol are futile, unheard.

People of today understand "the depths," even if they translate the concept into "acute anxiety," or normless fear. Perhaps I was too quick to listen too readily to people like Dilthey who assumed that moderns cannot identify with what the psalmists knew about sin. Dietrich Bonhoeffer in

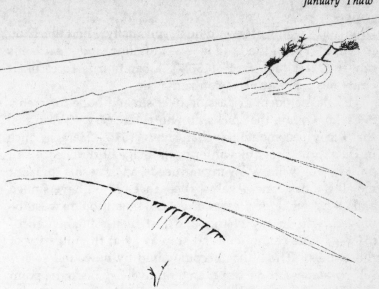

wartime Germany was too ready to relegate the depth experience of sin to intellectuals, those acutely anxious, or secularized Methodists. The image of "the depths" rings true for those who kept the company of ignoring fools but could not dismiss the notion of their own being responsible. The depths of the waters, fathoms deep, are ready to overwhelm, and yet I cry out. The psalmist surmises that one who is to hear *could* be engaged in bookkeeping and accounting, unable to look up and be distracted by a mere human plea for help. Of course, God has the right and power to do such accounting. But the crier has reasons to know that the call of a person in need interrupts the divine agenda.

Such a passage in a text makes sin sound ignorable and grace, easy. Other psalms will counter that kind of notion. For the moment, in the spirit of relief that we were seeking in January thaw, it is good to open a text that suggests a ready response. "I wait for the Lord with all my soul" (130: 5), "more eagerly than watchmen for the morning" (130:6).

Crouching, leaning forward next, spiritually, I find the Thou in range: "For in the Lord is love unfailing, and great is his power to set men free" (130:7). Liberation is forceful, it emits heat. The streams can run again.

The classic poem of passion over sin and hope for mercy is Psalm 51, one that picks up wintry imagery: "Wash me, that I may become whiter than snow" (51:7). Here, as once in Isaiah, the snow of winter is an image of innocence and purity. "For well I know my misdeeds, and my sins confront me all the day long. Against thee, thee only, I have sinned and done what displeases thee, so that thou mayest be proved right in thy charge and just in passing sentence" (51:3–4). One cannot cut and snip away at the integrity of those lines. "Thou" has become vivid by now, and so has self-awareness. If we can even tentatively come to the point of saying that beyond the offenses against the spouse, parent, child, lover, friend, neighbor, employee, there is a larger backdrop and it is personified: "against thee, thee only," we have now opened the possibility of finding a way out of the depths, straits, and chill. Sin against the creature finally violates the creator. Evil in the world is a sign of scorn for the agent and keeper of that world. These psalms address the wintry sort of spirituality and do not make the transit to grace easy. There is always a yes shrouded amid many noes, and spring is overlooked in the depth of winter. The psalm is explicit about the limits of summer and sunshine: "Thou hast hidden the truth in darkness" (51:6). The truth in this case is the mystery of sin, about which the psalmist can never write a philosophically satisfying explanation. He is only living out the terms of such evil. In the midst of the mystery and confusion, even there, especially there, "through this mystery thou dost teach me wisdom" (51:6).

Few lines do better than those at spelling out the spirituality of the psalms. Some passages, to be sure, allow for rooftop whooping, waving of hands, and dancing before the altar. Instruments are made available, and one then hears clapping and "Praise the Lord." But when the author turns basic about conception and birth, death and dying, and when the stage is bare, then, most clearly, truth comes still wrapped in darkness, wisdom comes *through* the mystery of sin.

After that passionate cry in the darkness and through the mystery, in the midst of the heart's winter, comes the prayer for thaw and warmth. "Let me hear the sounds of joy and gladness, let the bones dance which thou hast broken" (51: 8). The psalms are not designed to appeal to the self-indulgent who enjoy portraying themselves as most mean and miserable. They do not congratulate the wintry sort for knowing most about darkness and misery. The texts go along to the depths with such persons, but they do not leave victims there. The passage to the new way comes through divine response to prayer: "Create a pure heart in me, O God, and give me a new and steadfast spirit" (51:10), "revive in me the joy of thy deliverance and grant me a willing spirit to uphold me" (51:12). The new heart does not build on the old but replaces it. The Holy Spirit prayed for here is the divine presence that may appear on that horizon where other contemporaries have known only godlessness. The first hint of that presence brings "the joy of deliverance."

Near the end of this psalm the praying person recognizes that routine sacrifice has no effect and offers only the one thing that can bring change: "My sacrifice, O God, is a broken spirit; a wounded heart, O God, thou wilt not despise" (51:17). Brokenness and wounding do not occur in order to break human dignity but to open the heart so God can act.

Where the pure heart and the new creation occur, the psalmist begins to be separated from those who have not brought the sacrifice of sorrow for sin or desire for change. Whatever became of sin? It lives on, says Psalm 4, in the "many" who say, "If only we might be prosperous again! But the light of thy presence has fled from us, O Lord" (4:6). They have known the goods of earth but not the good of the Lord. They have looked for security in things, not in persons.

Without bragging and in a spirit of joy the writer can begin a contrast: "Yet in my heart thou hast put more happiness than they enjoyed when there was corn and wine in plenty" (4:7). The thaw and warmth may be episodic. More winter is ahead. But the psalmist knows the intrinsic value of the good day and the good gift. On the strength of these he leads modern pilgrims to face the return of a chill that follows January thaw, the silence that comes when winterbourne again temporarily ceases its flow.

7. The Season of Abandonment

THE THEME OF DERELICTION

Thus far we have usually been able to set the stage by first reflecting on the human condition. Now a psalm would open a world of possibility to address this condition; then a psalm must come first. We are to the point of dealing with those psalms of the second winter, psalms that speak boldly of abandonment by friends and by God. Here is the shock of dereliction. One pictures the worshiping person as a derelict ship abandoned on the rocks and to the winds and ice. Were it not in these scriptures the notion would seem to be too shocking to belong in the experience of the godly.

The abandoned person who excludes God from her horizon remains simply abandoned. Her story seems to end with simple dereliction. The psalmist, however, is able to face what it is to be derelict because of an often tested but still unshakable conviction that all the seasons of the heart, like all the seasons of nature, remain in the hands and mind of God. To this, Psalm 74 (verses 16 and 17) speaks: "The day is thine, and the night is thine also, thou hast fixed all the regions of the earth; summer and winter, thou didst create them both."

Even if the presence of God is not strong and vivid at the moment of this psalm, whoever approaches the next text does well to hold the possibility in mind that *God remains in control.* Without such a possibility, these psalms are utterly beyond us. We cannot endure them. To employ the wintry metaphor, there seem to be nothing but the winds or the silences of an eternal Arctic around and ahead of us. Each psalm brings its own rhythm. By the end there is something to affirm because of the reality of God. Along the way, however, there are no props except the remembered and hoped for presence of the God who sets the climate and the times, the rhythm of the seasons.

The sense of spiritual abandonment comes with such frequency in this prayerbook that all who believe in God must be ready to experience it. Despite preparations against it, this sense can rise against a person with resistless suddenness and fury. The questing soul finds that January thaw was but a postponement of the worse to come, like false dawn before new dark, or Indian summer after the first frost. Enjoy January thaw while it is here, says the mind; bask in the soul's new warmth. Soon a second, deeper winter threatens.

PHYSICAL SUFFERING AS REALITY AND METAPHOR

Sufferers of physical illness know that it has a way of working itself out with this rhythm of attack, relief, and new attack. Many a cancer patient after suffering the first attacks has addressed them through therapy and prayer. Then comes a period of partial relief. The disease goes into remission as the medications and radiation work their effect. The loved ones begin to hope again that all will be relatively well. The patient resumes a few activities. She is soon driving the auto again and, if not yet zestful enough to prepare meals, at least can enjoy some again. Before long the routines of life return: the punch of the time clock, checking in at the desk as well as with the doctor, enjoying an evening out. As the promise of warmer breezes attract, the patient with cancer in remission seeks a vacation and takes it. She sends postcards to friends back home. These speak of new health and, in measured terms, of hope.

Sometimes remission lasts for years. (There *may* be a cure!) Those who have observed the sequence for many a sufferer, however, know to keep a corner of their minds suspicious. This is the time for mental finger crossing. A person is wary, not in order to limit the joy of the warmed season but in order to prepare for what may and often must come. And it *can* come, choosing its own season. The malignant cells become active and overpowering. The vacation ends, the clock no longer clunks the beginning and end of a working day. The victim is back to the routine of therapy. The circle of friends and the praying congregation regather. Now they do best to light the candle and send their greeting cards. They begin again the little gestures of visiting and extending cheer in empathy. No one is deluded. This time the disease is back with a vengeance.

The friends may reach out in generosity, but the victim knows that they also have their lives to lead. There are limits to altruism. Few can tolerate a life that consists of nothing but the need to respond to gifts. Few lives have the luxury of knowing such sustained care. In the end, dying is one's own act. Even if one dies in company, the final trip is isolated, the pain is one's own experience. The squeeze of a loved one's hand cannot relieve pain after medication has lost its ability to help. The experience of approach to dying will get lonelier. Friends become exhausted, or patronizingly sick of someone's being sick, impatient with being patient, tired of playing the saintly and heroic roles of "being with."

Such friends may turn away in acts of ultimate cruelty and leave the dying one alone to face the night of silence. They close the door of disappointment on those who, in company, had once known hope. Most of those who were called friends, however, *were* friends, because they could be counted on never to move toward such cruelty. They simply run out of the ability to be spontaneous about identifying with someone else, to take into themselves the agony of nerves exposed, the plotlessness of pain that never stops. They have their own coffee pots to put on, their own pay-checks to draw, their own bright moments to celebrate. Such people cannot help but be tempted to turn their backs at some decisive stage. Even the most surrounded and sup-ported patient knows this, fears this.

Physical illness is only a metaphor for the spiritual dis-ease that afflicts those with a wintry sort of spirituality. Our present effort through a season is not to deal with the how-to of care and cure. Instead, we are facing the leanness and loneliness of soul. Whoever has gone through the winter season in that respect knows the rhythms of which we have just written.

THE DANGER OF SPIRITUAL RELAPSE

The classic works on spirituality prepare us for this second winter, each under its own metaphor. The Dark Night of the Soul knows the false dawn and then faces the darker night. Someone in or faced by the Cloud of Unknowing at times sees through its mists and follows the beckoning of the sun beyond it. Then, with sudden fury, the bleakest or blackest clouds re-form, but first they threaten, and then open in fierceness. The practice of the presence of God allows one in the midst of the kitchen pots and pans to be aware of nearness. Then, when the presence seems accessible, just as suddenly comes the second, more stark absence.

Modern therapy matches classic spirituality. Members of Alcoholics Anonymous know the dangers of relapse that follow the sense of gain. Surrounded by friends who support the victim after she "surrenders" and recognizes no hope without help, the alcoholic undertakes disciplines that lead to progress. She testifies to her temptations and partial, apparent victories. No longer must she physically avoid parties where alcohol is served. While she would never call herself cured, she is on a course toward steadiness and can begin to test herself.

Knowing better than to go to the New Year's Eve party where the gowns are cut low, the spirits are high, and the alcohol flows, she decides to tough it out in front of television at home. Far away from fellow Alcoholics Anonymous, who face their own private demons and support themselves with intimate circles of helpful friends, she is pounced upon by an unannounced enemy: self-pity. Self-pity comes wearing the mask of assurance. You deserve something, old girl. You had a good whole year. You won back respect and self-respect. You really showed those who said you would relapse. Let's see now, if that calls for a celebration, who would know that you kept hidden that little bit of vodka in a medicine bottle for a time like this? Why not just nip it a bit, since you know you have control and can stop when you want? The drug store is still open, and after the nip, well before midnight, you can make a pilgrimage for a new bottle for fresh sustenance. New Year's Day breaks on a sodden victim, derelict, abandoned, alone.

Even Alcoholics Anonymous, spiritual as it may be, has a physical and medical aspect that sets it apart from the soul search. The serious believer knows that the spiritual life does not sustain itself without practice. He sets up a discipline. Each day, as regularly as he swims or plays racquetball, this year he resolves to take care of the heart and its needs. He will take pains to be less busy. The time has come for him to be attentive to the quiet voices within and not only to the agenda and pressures from without. Sacred texts are available. Inspired and saintly people who knew that without discipline there could be no going into depths wrote them. Reading these texts should help. There must be pilgrimages to zones where the sacred impinges on the mundane. A candle burns in the temple. A person with an eye fixed on its glow can imagine himself into the Presence. Grace reaches out in the sacred acts and sacraments, and the seeker will be there to be reached and grasped. So go the resolves.

When the discipline is most rewarding

In the rhythm of response to those resolves, the January thaw in the heart's winter has an almost assured place. Those who follow a discipline find that very soon they do make some progress. Without too much effort, they feel the benefits of having set aside hours and places for quiet reverence. In this respect, the spiritual discipline does not differ too much from what occurs in the first few guitar or sketching lessons. After the silence and then anarchy of first plunkings, one soon comes to know the satisfaction of playing the scales and then some tunes. After the disorder of the chalk box and the challenge of the blank drawing pad, ordering of lines and colors occurs as the teacher in the first and second of the "ten easy lessons" imparts the rudiments of drawing. "I am on the way," says the future Segovia or Matisse. At last a method connects with the promise of a previously undiscovered genius. It is a delight to breathe an "aha!" during the period of catching on.

In lesson three the rules of the game suddenly change. The mentor is not constantly at the side. He withdraws and sends the strummer and plunker home to endless sequences of numbing exercises. The teacher cannot look over a shoulder at the easel all the time. Most of what happens during development is too drab. The pace of second-stage learning is too unpromising to make tutorial presence and time valuable. You are on your own, dear student, and you know it. In lesson three those who wanted to play on Saturday or paint on Sunday become separated from those who will finish the course. Even those who want to finish, however, come to the barren periods when the discipline is as high as the motivation is low. The slump sets in.

So it is in the spiritual life, which admits of no "ten easy lessons," and allows for no simple step-by-step progression toward the vision of God. There especially, each disciple leads a different life. Any of a billion particulars can change the course of the soul search. Winds of winter come from corners of the mind where everything once seemed well banked and snow fenced. Suddenly there is drift, the disorientation of the "white out," the temptation to lie down in the illusorily warm and inviting snowbank, where a pilgrim may succumb and die. In the drift the seeker reaches out to find that this far out on the frontier of the soul the companions have gone on a different course. You are left alone. A soliloquy follows: *There was a guide, wasn't there? Wasn't there a guide, a Guide? Where is this Guide? Which way is north? Why are there no more lights in cottage windows? Why can't I find my compass? Did I bring one? Is there a north? Is there a— Is there— Is?—?*

131

The story of jesus' abandonment

"Thou hast fixed all the regions of the earth; summer and winter, thou didst create them both" (74:17). It seems like cheating to bring back this text with its quiet response to the Presence. Like the Christian who is ready to celebrate the banquet of fulfillment without drinking the cup of suffering, the person who does not take abandonment seriously because of the knowledge of the Presence lives superficially. Some readers of the Good Friday story, in which Jesus dies, cheat, because, knowing the Easter outcome, they do not allow for Jesus' own sense of abandonment at the crucial stage. The Christian story has a happy ending, it is said, so the chapters of the plot are all endurable along the way. Yet that is precisely not the way they unfold in the biblical narratives.

The biblical narratives bring up mysteries they only address but never fully unfold. They tell that God wanted to be so close to the human race that Jesus took on the conditions of humanity and left behind the securities of identification with God. Whatever that meant to Christian minds

132

when it was written, it has to be partially obscure to people who come at the story from a distance and cannot even conceive of themes like "the pre-existence of the Logos," the divine word that takes flesh in Christ. To such minds—is not yours, like mine, one of them?—the uncluttered Gospel story that occurs on the soil of a holy land is the only true beginning place.

In that story even Jesus, the designated representative of the Divine One and Way knows a remission followed by new onslaught, the second winter after the January thaw. In those puzzling Gospel accounts the circle of Gospel preachers and writers never seems to understand them. Then momentarily, someone catches on. The authors do not linger to flatter those who grasp the meanings. In the Gospel of Mark, a few lines after Peter quoted the correct words about who Jesus was as divine messenger, this same Peter was condemned as "Satan," invited to begone for getting it all wrong. The disciples sleep under trees in gardens while their comrade Jesus sweats blood in an agony artists have tried to catch, but only the agonized one himself could endure.

Dereliction: does this happen to the chosen one? Is his career of saving finally to end in ashes, the dust, or the spindrift snows? Abandonment: in this story, certainly, someone is only playing games, "just kidding." Jesus only had to go through the motions and suffer temporary inconvenience as they drove spikes through his wrist and taunted him while imparting pain. Didn't he? Anyone can stand a little pain in the wrist, if paradise is to open later in the day. And who cares what the scorners say during their brief day? It will pass, and the victim on the tree will rise to begin the New Creation. Easy does it. Easy.

All I need to do, says the bearer of a summery sort of spirituality, is to hear that Good Friday story and keep the happy Easter ending in view. Let me get angry at Romans as instruments, Jews as taunters, myself as sinful neglecter. That strategy allows for a bit of scapegoating or masochism. Such acts and emotions are harmless and passing, however. In the end, Romans, Jews, and I are hardly responsible for a gross crime. We are only agents of a plot that ends well. Abandonment? A game of charades. The divine child, Jesus, grows up and takes a role. Guess what I am playing now? The game of D-e-r-e-l-i-c-t-i-o-n. Break it into syllables. Act out "diary" for "dere" and "lick" and "shun" and you get dereliction. Before the other side guesses the word, Jesus will be off the cross, resting in the tomb, risen to whiteness and glory. And we all live happily ever after.

If a person rehears the story that way, it comes off as better adventure and entertainment, but this has nothing to do with the second winter in the soul. After the melting, the paths seemed clear again, but then they drifted shut. After the warming, the winterers opened their jackets and left the heaviest clothes back at the inn. Then came the most perilous windchill.

At three in the morning comes a realization. My family is off nurturing their needs with untroubled sleep, and I have the nightmare. Who has a moral claim to trouble them as I go to the bathroom and interrupt the quiet and the darkness? Suddenly the universe is larger and darker than before. I, the thinking reed, am smaller and more alone than the genius Pascal expected me to be. Nothing, no one cares. I go off into the darkness, probably not even bothering to reflect on the Jesus story of dereliction and abandonment. Happy endings don't fix themselves in the mind during the three in the morning upset.

Then, in the soul's dark night and the heart's deep winter, comes the recall of a shriek or a groan more intense than all the others. The quotation on the cross comes from the psalms, and I can never let it go: *"My God, my God, why hast thou forsaken me?"* There is more, still unuttered but still belonging to the context of the text. Why art thou "so far from saving me, from heeding my groans?" (22:1). This becomes too much for the believer to take. That *she* can be forsaken is endurable, because of the happy ending to come. But that *He* is abandoned? Quickly: we need an explanation.

Some commentators rush to help. Their counsel seems inert on the pages of leatherbound, gilt-edged, gold-stamped library books. Who will know to consult them? But they have their wisdom, and they want to be humane. They are scholars and know something I might not notice without their help. Someone has taught them about ritual and quotation. It is their agenda to "make things come out right" when the scripture texts leave moderns too puzzled and amazed. Some of them have found out how to make this incident come out right, to let the happy ending come soon enough to do Jesus and the reader some good.

Jesus was only quoting. Only quoting, they say. And who quotes a text without drawing on a context? Cite anything from the Gettysburg Address or the Sermon on the Mount and to hearers or readers it connotes a setting in which it was first spoken or recorded. They can draw on any other part of the same address or sermon. So it is with the psalms. The Jewish boy Jesus was already wise enough at age twelve to engage the doctors and scholars in scriptures. Now in his thirties, on the cross, he has a richer store of biblical lore. He knows these psalms from memory.

On those terms, Jesus knows this psalm. It is part of the liturgy, say these commentators. The psalms are the Jewish prayerbook in synagogue and home alike. No one quotes the beginning of Psalm 22 without implying its end, its happy ending. Remember? Happiness must come at all costs, including the cost of interrupting the plot and using the ending to inform the minds of characters at mid-plot. How does

Psalm 22 proceed? "But do not remain so far away, O Lord; O my help, hasten to my aid" (22:19). Even more positive verses are to follow. So long as the crier keeps the Thou before the I, expecting the possibility of deliverance, there is deliverance. The drift does not seem overpowering and the chill is not deadening.

The commentators *may* be right. But what they offer seems to have little to do with agonies in the garden, the drinking of bitter cups, or the expectation of Easter dawn. If the bright ending is known to be ahead, then all that the pious can say to Jesus is, "There, there, don't cry (out); this will only hurt a little while." What would follow is no more an ordeal—except for possibly more intense physical pain—than a dental chair whose terrors are lessened by high-speed drills and novocaine. Offer him vinegar mixed with gall on a sponge and long stick, for relief.

Physical pain was not the point. Spiritual abandonment was. The psalm in question does not hurry to the springtime of deliverance. It walks the reader through the second winter of forsakenness. In this plot, the point is precisely that Jesus does experience abandonment. *"My God, my God, why hast thou forsaken me?"*

When I am henceforth lost in the wintry night, alone, I identify exactly with a cry already uttered: "O my god, I cry in the day-time but thou dost not answer, in the night I cry but get no respite" (22:2). The world in front of this text opens to me the possibility that by uttering the prayer, a prayer of aloneness, I am not only alone. Someone in whom I trust has shouted it out before, in worse circumstances. What is more, Jesus cried out because a pledge seemed to be broken, and that seemingly was turning to reality. *Because* it seemed so, it *was* being broken. He was not supposed to be abandoned, yet he was abandoned. "The cry of dereliction": under that term his shout enters the list of classic phrases.

There are derelict ships and there was a derelict Son of God.

If the Jesus remembered in the Gospel was drawing on more of this psalm than one line, he was recalling a story. Then it appears both as irony and as appeal. Irony: You said you *would* help, because you *did* help. Appeal: Because you helped others, help me. "Thou art he whose praises Israel sings. In thee our fathers put their trust; they trusted, and thou didst rescue them. Unto thee they cried and were delivered" (22:3–5).

The world that opens here then quickly closes itself again. "But I am a worm, not a man, abused by all men, scorned by the people" (22:6). The Gospel writers who tell the story of the abandoned one's death seem to be using the psalm as a template. Here is the pattern, and the passersby in the story of Jesus' crucifixion live it all out: "All who see me jeer at me, make mouths at me and wag their heads: 'He threw himself on the Lord for rescue; let the Lord deliver him, for he holds him dear!' " (22:7–8).

The winter wanderer in the drift tries all the strategies as he seeks direction. Where is the Guide for this pilgrimage? He reminds the Guide that His reputation is at stake. People make fun of those who in trust staked everything on that reputation. He insists on the reality: they have a *right* to! The reputation for leadership was ill deserved. The medieval artists used their imaginations to describe the terrors of this particular hell. They still did not match the spiritual inward dryness: "I am laid low in the dust of death" (22:15).

A LANGUAGE OF TRUST ERUPTS

A new commentary before me is more helpful than the older pious ones that asked me not to take dereliction seriously because it was only part of that plot with the happy ending. This book instead reminds me that for once the psalmist in asking why is not really looking for answers. That stage is past, that part of the game is over. This now is the cry of despair that goes beyond disappointment. Over against it, the language of trust that erupts in the middle of the text almost seems misplaced; three times in two verses Israel's ancient trust is mentioned. Once upon a time not everyone was abandoned; why am I, now?

The worst sense of dereliction comes when others enter the scene in order to taunt. They live by their doctrines and philosophies. That is why they have credentials to scorn, "He threw himself on the Lord for rescue"; let the Lord rescue him. They ask, Why should anyone be abandoned to illness or spiritual agony unless she deserved it? God is good, so suffering has to be punishment.

This fresh commentary then plays a little trick. Whereas it treats most psalms in continuity, as one piece, this one gets chopped in two. First comes the text of the psalm and then the commentary. One thinks it all ends at verse 21 where there has been as yet no language but a cry. Then I turn the page, and there follow verses 22–31, the ones that emboldened the commentators who said: The abandoned one is only quoting; the psalm ends upbeat. And it does. "I will declare thy fame to my brethren; I will praise thee in the midst of the assembly" (22:22). The congregation regathers. "Let all the ends of the earth remember and turn again to the Lord" (22:27).

Even these bright passages carry along with them reminders of realities that were vivid to the psalmist but convey something that the impatient are eager to suppress. Summery spirituality welcomes the springtime of these lines, but it overlooks a reminder that for the psalmist spring is not eternal and the worshiper is not naturally immortal. Realism and wintriness are recurrent. "How can those buried in the earth do him homage, how can those who go down to the grave bow before him?" (22:29).

Whoever looks for simplistically positive philosophies of life has to slide past such verses. They served the writer well. For now, for now at least, God owes it to the victim and the world to keep him alive, so that there can still be praise. The lines serve the hungerer for the eternal quality of life less well. All they do is remind that praise lasts for a day longer, and *then* comes the silence and the chill. Still, in this darkness one grasps for any light: "But I shall live for his sake, my posterity shall serve him" (22:29–30). A kind of extension if not immortality informs the end: "This shall be told of the Lord to future generations; and they shall justify him, declaring to a people yet unborn that this was his doing" (22:30–31).

Those lines do catch one, inspiring a gasp as when one comes upon winter light. They do not make up a proof for the existence of God. They do nothing to offer a philosophically rewarding answer to the problem of evil. It is possible to write them off as illusion. Perhaps I project my own needs for a trustworthy universe far enough ahead to get the response: a trustworthy God *is* behind it all. Yet, for all the reserve clauses included and for all the suspicions around, even in the second winter a remarkable observation haunts and thrills. It *is* true: generations yet unborn in the psalmist's imagining have now been born and are doing the praising and trusting. Those who trusted, even in abandonment, were not denied. The crucified victim was the *only* forsaken one, the true derelict. The rest of us die in company, in *his* company. God certified his gift and his act and "raised him up." Never again is aloneness to be so stark for others.

Dereliction and abandonment in the rhythms of life

After the astonishing recognition of trust through the passage of time, it would be tempting to close the Book of Psalms, take the rest of the day off, and not let thoughts of

dereliction cross the mind again. But come they will. It is
profitable, therefore, for someone under spiritual discipline
to turn the pages and see how else the second wintriness
afflicts. The cries of dereliction are not rare punctuations of
psalmic serenity. They always have their assured place *before*
anyone can say yes in trust.

The world in front of the text presents more of the wintry
landscape in combined Psalms 42–43, a song of great beauty
and longing. "Day and night, tears are my food; 'Where is
your God?' they ask me all day long" (42:3). When one
encounters such a psalm, it is hard to give privileged place
to the summery sorts who allow for no shadow or ice in the
terrain of faith. Without doubt they pick up on a biblical
theme, but they do it an injustice if they claim that the Bible
only addresses their tropical kind of praise.

Where is winterbourne, for the starving deer? "As a hind
longs for the running streams, so do I long for thee, O God.
With my whole being I thirst for God, the living God"
(42:1–2). In a grim gallows-humored way, it is almost amus-
ing to see this writer revisit memories as if in appeal to the
God who is now so remote. "As I pour out my soul in
distress, I call to mind how I marched in the ranks of the
great to the house of God, among exultant shouts of praise,
the clamour of the pilgrims" (42:4). *Then* were the good old
days, and *those* were the good old boys and girls, but now
they are gone, and I am "groaning in my distress" (42:5),
"sunk in misery" (42:6).

Israel today advertises ski country, isolated in its north-
east at Mount Hermon. The psalm knows that geography:
"I am sunk in misery, therefore will I remember thee, though
from the Hermons . . . deep calls to deep in the roar of thy
cataracts, and all thy waves, all thy breakers, pass over me"
(42:6–7). On the mountain far from Jerusalem in the fast-
nesses of snowy wilderness the people felt most isolated.

Now my heart is in such a circumstance. Abandonment is now nightmare: under the earth, thought the psalmist, were limitless stores of dark water. God opened the highest mountains and let these rush upon the victim: deep calls to deep, and deep is deadly.

The poets today do not do as well with dereliction as this ancient did. They reach for words from the modern landscape and depict terror, but none is so vivid for the mind of today as those torrents must have been for the person who stood in the way then. The absence of dams and the presence of mythical explanations more horrible than those that geologists and weather people today provide must have induced awe. Yet few poets today are able to summon the first words of affirmation that psalmists could embed in these psalms of abandonment.

The modern of whom Karl Rahner spoke, who excludes God from the horizon of consciousness, is not ready for the constancy of trust in the psalms. In the midst of deeps unimaginable today, there are, if not heights, still some rocks on which to stand. "Yet I will wait for God" (42:5). More surprisingly, "The Lord makes his unfailing love shine forth alike by day and night" (42:8). Repeatedly: "I will praise him continually, my deliverer, my God" (42:5,11; 43:5). These lines are risks, because they seem remote in our contemporary experience. Abandonment comes now because God is silent, absent, eclipsed. Praise came then because God was alive, was potentially a speaker, ready as a presence. To bring up the risks of these potential embarrassments is exactly the point of our kind of reading. The world in front of the text of psalms like these does *not* abandon us to abandonment. It discloses ways of being in the world that remain possibilities in any age or circumstance. Many who prayed such psalms in the face of disease, dereliction, or mortality have found their trust confirmed. This fact does not make trusting easy, but it does point to the possibility of trust. It becomes our winter light.

MIXING THE "YESES" WITH SILENCE

Soon one becomes accustomed to a startling language, one that is unfamiliar in our day and therefore perhaps is able to alter our opinions. Today the choice seems to be either dereliction—waiting for No One—*or* summery spirituality, which does not allow for honest searching of the lonely heart. All these psalms mix the two, as if for the wintry trip one needs extra stores of warmth and energy. Psalm 13 four times asks, "How long?" How long will the Lord "quite forget me" (13:1) and hide the divine face? How long "must I suffer anguish in my soul, grief in my heart" (13:2) and thus wintriness of spirit? "How long shall my enemy lord it over me?" (13:2) The modern re-utters the "How longs" but does not let the later lines speak: "My heart shall rejoice, for thou hast set me free. I will sing to the Lord, who has granted all my desire" (13:5–6). To close with such lines may sound disruptive, out of tune. Yet the psalmist had *some* reason to speak thus.

Psalm after psalm tumbles open with themes like these. Sometimes they sound trivial, as if a mere slight by a friend is big enough to disturb the universe. Against the background of the experience of abandonment, such a slight does signal a problem in the larger world. "My friends shudder at me; when they see me in the street they turn quickly away" (31:11). At times a person is ready to turn cynical and say, And well they might. You aren't exactly a cheery person with whom people will want to keep company. You would brighten the scene by staying hidden. Take a pill to get out of your misery. Brighten up before you reappear. We have our own loads to carry. What makes you special? So it could be until it occurs to the reader that the psalmist is speaking in images for others, for people of many personalities. "I am forgotten, like a dead man out of mind; I have come to be like something lost" (31:12).

The idea dawns that these psalms are supposed to sound like Friedrich Heiler's spontaneous cries from the heart. Yet as one reads more and more in the text, they take on a ritualized, almost routine, character. They organize passion into patterns that produce a certain expectation among readers. Curiously, they cause wonder because of the unexpectedness of such endings in ancient time. Would Jean-Paul Sartre, Samuel Beckett, or the nihilists who place the characters on stage in our time risk facing critics with texts that open two worlds in the extreme today? Yet the psalms do create a world of plausibility *and* remain promising for the ages. They seem to be written so that those of us with a narrower range of experience can also participate. New generations can find a language long forgotten from when "deep calls unto deep."

THE NEED FOR COMMUNITY

One reason the psalms allow for hope and affirming in the midst of abandonment's second winter is their collective character. The modern spiritual discipline so often calls upon entrepreneurship and is a lonely experience. The psalms teach their readers to identify again with a community of worshippers. Few poets today can match them in the use of the "I." Confessional poetry today sounds simpering by contrast with the terror of the abandoned "I" of these psalms. The psalms also readily slip into a more helpful "we," even in the passages of lament and complaint. "We cannot see what lies before us, we have no prophet now; we have no one who knows how long this is to last" (74:9). This plural dimension introduces a new note for the diagnostician of fear.

People can endure some boredom if they can also anticipate Saturday night orgy, summer vacation, graduation, or the end of a dreary job. They can endure suffering, and most heroes have done so, if there is the possibility of rescue at the end. Not to be able to look into the future and know what is ahead is what numbs victims. "We have no prophet now."

Where there was no prophet, there was a historian or reporter. In cases like these, hope is much like remembering. Recall can function as hope so long as God is trustworthy. The psalm in effect makes its appeal by reminding the trusted one of past occasions for trust. Here is where we read that God "hast fixed all the regions of the earth; summer and winter, thou didst create them both" (74:17). If there is a cry, "Why hast thou cast us off, O God? Is it for ever?" (74:1), there is also a reminder, "Remember the assembly of thy people, taken long since for thy own" (74:2). The appeal is to God's character and promise. The psalmist assumes that if they remember all of this, the gathered people will prosper against the enemies of God.

Such quieter appeals do not help us forget the frequent times in which the psalms argue with God. In them there is room for anger and accusations. Rage may not always be therapeutic, but it is often natural. "O God, thou hast cast us off and broken us; thou hast been angry and rebuked us cruelly" (60:1). "Thou hast made thy people drunk with a bitter draught, thou hast given us wine that makes us stagger" (60:3). This opposes the reminders of a God of promise. A fateful 'since' is in the assumption: "Since thou, O God, hast abandoned us" who can guide? (60:10). In the quaint terms of the psalms such expression risks giving God the idea that there is no basis for trust. Act in character, O God, this seems to say, and we will remain abandoned. Yet even here there is a freshet of promised spring: "for deliverance by man is a vain hope," but with God's help "we shall do valiantly" (60:11, 12).

Sometimes psalmists come close to using the voice of modern reckoning. In one of the dereliction songs we hear: "I will set my ear to catch the moral of the story and tell on the harp how I read the riddle" (49:4). At this point it is reassuring to hear that we are not alone in finding injustice to be a mystery. Why the harp? No doubt there is a connection between the search for wisdom through inspiration and the act of singing. It is rare, almost unheard of, in biblical literature for the musical instrument to be an aid to riddle solving. The poetic context shows that where philosophy gives out, inspiration begins. What cannot be explained can be addressed, at least in song. Lines like these in any case are attractive because they bridge some of the distance between then and now, text and reader; the ancients who prayed the psalms did not know everything, either!

Dereliction is never far off, "Save me, O God; for the

waters have risen up to my neck. I sink in muddy depths and have no foothold; I am swept into deep water" (69:1), "I am wearied with crying out" (69:3). This time the abandonment gets even closer than the circle of friends. "I have become a stranger to my brothers, an alien to my own mother's sons" (69:8). Yet all that the writer can ask for is that "no abyss swallow me up, no deep close over me" (69:15). Then, almost in stereotype but still with a surprise that offers its own power, we read: "Answer me, O Lord, in the goodness of thy unfailing love, turn towards me in thy great affection" (69:16). Again, the risk of such psalms is apparent because they do not offer a second prop. Neither reasoning friends nor mothers' sons will rescue. Only the character of God endures for support.

Even that character of God seems absent at one turn in the psalms. We have seen it being included in the collection as a sign of biblical realism. Finally, there is no glossing over reality, no relief for reasons of public relations. Those of us who wish to make the transit through the heart's winter can take no refuge from it. Psalm 88 speaks of lament and woes, of abyss, dark places, depths. "I am in prison and cannot escape" (88:8). Beyond it all lurks the abode of the dead. "Shall their company rise up and praise thee? Will they speak of the faithful love in the grave, of thy sure help in the place of Destruction?" (88:10–11).

Recall of personal biography is no help in this wintry heartscape. "I have suffered from boyhood and come near to death; I have borne thy terrors, I cower beneath thy blows" (88:15). "Thou hast taken lover and friend far from me, and parted me from my companions" (88:18). This kind of word in scripture alienates the simple positive thinker and puzzles the commentators: maybe the end of the psalm is missing? We get no clue to that. Instead it stands as a reminder that some veils are so thick as to be impenetrable, some clouds so dark that they cannot but lead to storm. If there is to be a Yes beyond this psalm, we have traversed the worst.

THE CRY FOR HELP AS THE TURN TO THE YES

The turn toward the Yes necessarily begins with a new cry for help, a bid for a hearing. "Be not deaf to my cry, lest, if thou answer me with silence, I become like those who go down to the abyss" (28:1). Such a life implies a chance to establish connection again with God, the source of trust. When the meditator moves from "since" God is not responding to "if" God is silent, the world that opens before his text offers new possibilities. Now comes dazzle and dance: "The Lord is my strength, my shield, in him my heart trusts; so I am sustained, and my heart leaps for joy, and I praise him with my whole body" (28:7).

Such psalms begin to sound like contests with God. They speak to the heart of those who have carried on an argument with the silence. Why, O God, after a remission of disease, is it allowed to come back relentlessly until malign cells kill? Why, O Lord, after the victim of heart disease has begun to walk must a second attack fell her? Why, O Hidden One, after alcoholics or other addicts have known victories, must there come a moment when, off guard, they lapse? Why, O Silence, when one has moved through many stages of spiritual discipline, should there be a sudden drying up of the spirit? Why, O Absence, when the cry is most intense is the silence most stunning? The passionate heart searches for answers.

Psalm 44 carries this spirit. "In God have we gloried all day long, and we will praise thy name for ever" (44:8). To that point the prayer is conventional, since it is a reminder of God's own character and past deeds. Then comes an "instead," in which God plays unfairly. "But now thou hast

147

rejected and humbled us. . . . Thou hast given us up to be butchered like sheep. . . . Thou hast sold thy people for next to nothing and had no profit from the sale. . . . Thou hast made us a byword among the nations, . . . so my disgrace confronts me all day long, and I am covered with shame" (44:9–15). The concern is collective, for the people of Israel. The voice is personal. Shame finally falls on the person who prays.

Instead of giving up, however, Israel's psalmist keeps the context going. "All this has befallen us, but we do not forget thee and have not betrayed thy covenant; we have not gone back on our purpose" (44:17–18). This may not be the highest form of theology, because it suggests tit-for-tat transactions. It carries an endearing note, however, for this is the kind of honesty to which an earnest praying person finally admits. God, we are keeping our part of the bargain. What happened to you? "Because of thee we are done to death all day long, and are treated as sheep for slaughter" (44:22). Finally no enemy or fate is responsible. An absentee God is. There follows an almost humorous, certainly sardonic nudge, in the context of an anthology whose other pages make fun of nations whose gods are asleep. "Bestir thyself, Lord; why dost thou sleep? Awake, do not reject us for ever" (44:23). Finally, there is only one appeal: "For thy love's sake set us free" (44:26).

All these psalms except Psalm 88 lead toward an open future. In the face of the abyss, the psalmist finds reasons to affirm. The commentators whom we took too lightly when dealing with Psalm 22 were perhaps being more helpful than we gave them credit for. They did write in the spirit of the psalm book as a whole. Precisely in the context of those psalms where passions are most intense, the depths most threatening, the winters longest and most cold —there it is that the Yes of an awakening, responsive God is noticed. That suggestion raises another problem. What of the seeker for whom winter has gone on too long? What of the horizon so vacant of sacred presence that one forgets to look there? And when the Yes comes, what if the winterer has wearied and does not know any longer to care to bring forth a responsive Yes? The psalms have words for those situations, too, and they remain to be dealt with in the heart's long winter.

8. Winterfallow: Patience
for Community and Hope

A FALLOW TIME AS PROMISE

The seasons of the heart in our extended image parallel the
seasons of the year. The winterward heart moves to solstice
with the stark sense that, tilted too far from its sun, it will
chill. Far from marking a turn toward warmth, the season
after solstice is one of freeze: the soul knows that not all
nature is sleeping. Death pervades. At times wintertide
brings a January thaw, or the winterbourne stream breaks
out of the hard chalk understrata of life. Yet these are not
signs of a spring coming but a mere break for relief before
there comes a second, deepest winter.

A wintry sort of spirituality in the Christian context develops with the knowledge of a forthcoming springtime in the heart. Yet such a spirituality also has to move within the setting of a wintriness that remains as an aspect of being. Not all awakenings, then, rely upon the rhythms of the year. In the midst of winter, one can undertake acts that represent future promise.

The farmer shows his intentions by deciding to winterfallow a field. A fallow plot of ground is left unseeded, "not pregnant," is given its rest. The winterfallowed heart remains within the context of winter. Yet even the fallow field represents a kind of promise. Someone for a purpose has taken care not to seed. Seeded, cropped fields are busy. As their good seeds burst, so do their weeds. Rain and sun, cultivator and harrow and reaper, tramp of boot and peck of birds all agitate them. They may produce rich yield.

The believer moved by a wintry sort of spirituality may choose the fallow heart with good purpose. It may be that she is not ready for the grain or fruit, not able to cope with bounty. The summery sort of piety that advertises itself in the contemporary world is full of instant promise. Believe this evangelist and in a half hour of television time you can be converted. Send money to this healer and your cancer cells will disappear; you will walk in health. Buy the book of this psychologist and you will have success. Material goods will come to you and you will have "the abundant life."

The psalms do allow for such bounty. It is not hard to find passages of astonishing richness, sections of the anthology that celebrate the bursting forth of nature under the divine hand. Thus Psalm 65 speaks to God: "Thou dost visit the earth and give it abundance, as often as thou dost enrich it with the waters of heaven, brimming in their channels" (65:9). "Thou dost crown the year with thy good gifts and the palm-trees drip with sweet juice; the pastures in the wild are rich with blessing and the hills wreathed in happiness, the meadows are clothed with sheep and the valleys mantled in corn, so that they shout, they break into song" (65:11–13).

So long as such texts confront us with a world of possibility, it would be foolish, even alien to integrity, to say that the heart will never know summer or sunshine. If even the sere and drab pastures can erupt with produce until they have to "shout [and] break into song," then the promise to the soul of humans is doubly rich. They, too, shall dance. For that reason summery sorts of piety should not be seen as inauthentic or second-rate. They simply are not to be privileged. They have no monopoly on the ways of the heart or, from the psalmists' point of view, the ways of God toward the heart.

The winterfallowed heart readies itself for gifts whenever they come. Conversion, healing, or success and prosperity can be the result of psychological techniques. One can make them part of an almost automatic, even commercial, transaction. When these gifts come in such modes, they can turn the heart *from* God, for in their attractiveness they come to be pursued and cherished for their own sake. Then the gift alone is vivid whereas the hand of the Giver recedes. As the hand is forgotten, so is the Giver. The recipient remains rich in things, impoverished in spirit.

GOD SENT LEANNESS INTO THEIR SOUL

The psalmist knew about the hazards of such lures in the history of Israel. In Psalm 106 he sings of the great things God did. "It is good to give thanks to the Lord; for his love endures for ever." Then came a recall of the mighty deeds to a people who "sinned like our forefathers." These fathers took no account of God's marvels, they rebelled by the Red

Sea, yet God delivered them for his name's sake. "He led his people through the deeps as through the wilderness." Delivered, "they believed his promises and sang praises to him" (106:1–12).

The psalm does not leave them there in the land of milk and honey and corn, where the very fields would "shout" and "break into song." They had their promises fulfilled. The material products and military victories should have satisfied them. Then came the terrifying sense that something had gone wrong in their history and hearts. The psalmist introduces one of those phrases that begins "but . . ." They believed, they sang praises, *'but* they quickly forgot all he had done and would not wait to hear his counsel" (106:13). Here, as so often, "waiting," the key element in a wintry sort of spirituality, received no premium. They were impatient, and their story took a strange turn.

"Their greed was insatiable in the wilderness, they tried God's patience in the desert" (106:14). They were in a hurry to get the gifts and goods, impatient for God to work out a calendar appropriate to their needs. So, "he gave them what they asked but sent a wasting sickness among them" (106: 15).

One hundred times a person can read such a psalm line and it opens nothing new. The one hundred and first time, it can disclose what had remained hidden in it. The reference in this psalm is to the eleventh chapter of Numbers, a tale worth recounting in the context of winterfallow. At Taberah in the wilderness, "the rabble that was among them had a strong craving" (RSV). And the people of Israel wept again and said, "O that we had meat to eat! We remember the fish we ate in Egypt for nothing, the cucumbers, the melons, the leeks, the onion, and the garlic." The whole menu from their slavedays' tables seemed succulent in retrospect. "But now our strength is dried up, and there is nothing at all but this manna to look at." Manna was bland. The cake they made of it "was like the taste of cakes baked with oil." Anyone who remembered leeks and garlic would be understandably tempted to weary of manna cakes.

Moses thereupon engaged in shuttle diplomacy between impatient Israel and its Lord. "I am not able to carry all this people alone, the burden is too heavy for me. If thou wilt deal thus with me, kill me at once, if I find favor in thy sight, that I may not see my wretchedness." And the same Lord who could bless the hills until they shouted and sang responded with a promise of meat. Israel should eat it for "a whole month, until it comes out at your nostrils and becomes loathsome to you," because Israel had rejected the Lord. The cry, "Why did we come forth out of Egypt?" was a repudiation of all the acts of deliverance. The Lord was rejected. Moses paid no attention to the divine petulance and worried about practical problems. He desired the month's worth of meat no matter what satiety and crapulence would follow the orgy.

Leave it to the Lord. "Is the Lord's hand shortened? Now you shall see whether my word will come true or not." So the Lord sent a great wind, and it brought quail from the sea and even arranged to "let them fall beside the camp," a day's journey's worth in each direction, two cubits—three feet—deep. Refrigeration, we must assume, was a problem and spoilage a threat, but the people had what they wanted: goods, meat. "And the people rose all that day, and all night, and all the next day, and gathered the quails." The storyteller saw no reason for economy of detail. Only by repetition and grossness could he convey the sense of greed.

"While the meat was yet between their teeth, before it was consumed, the anger of the Lord smote the people with a very great plague." In one of those anticlimactic touches that impart realism to a saga, the author adds that they named the place Kibroth-hattaavah, "because there they buried the people who had the craving." Even more anticlimactically, "the people journeyed to Hazeroth."

The psalm spiritualizes the story, without revisiting the detail. Now was not the time to discuss ptomaine in a clinical sense. The text existed to remind people of a moment as awesome and horrible in their history as the plague and black death were in the recall of medieval Europeans. The plague was a wasting disease. People with full stomachs and bowels suddenly lost their taste for food and disgorged what they already had eaten. The full were seen to be wasting away; those gifted with the fat of the land ended up lean.

For me, the one hundred and first reading came after a mental repeal of the revised modern translations, which speak of the moment when "he gave them what they asked but sent a wasting sickness" (106:15), or in another translation, a "wasting disease." Here was a case where the archaic King James Version illuminated the spiritual meaning, whether the old translation was fully appropriate or not. *"And he gave them their request; but sent leanness into their soul"* (106:15).

"He sent leanness . . ." David Head made a whole prayerbook "for the natural man" out of this theme, showing that one can have the goods—conversion, healing, prosperity—and still possess an impoverished and wasting spirit. Manna had served the people of Israel better than the garlic and leeks of their enslavement days in Egypt or the bounty of quail sent them when they complained. Living with manna demanded patience, and the people had to wait upon the Lord for it. They assumed that life owed them more abundance and variety and fastened on the meaning of fullness and fatness.

APATHY, ANOMIE, ACCEDIE

The fallow heart is to learn the disciplines of patience and waiting and to find in these an integrity in relation to God. Yet even the stillness of wilderness life and the spare landscape of winter in the heart by themselves do not assure that the hand of the giver, the source of life, will be recognized. The psalms devote themselves considerably to this issue. The sated soul needs a different kind of leanness, a "clean heart" and a right spirit. In the late winter of the heart's season, there is need for an "unseeded, uncropped" and "not pregnant" time, so that when there is again to be a seeding, the soil will be ready.

In the face of summery spirituality and its exuberance, the wintry sort seems to come up dry. A reader has to call up the words from ancient and medieval times, words dictionary writers have marked "obsolete." Now, in the revisions, they see such words returned to active use. *Apatheia,* "apathy": being neither for nor against the abundance poured out on an already full life. The preacher may rave the good news and rant the terrors of God; the church doors may open and the eucharistic banquet be set; the choirs may shout and sing as fields never could. Yet if the gifts are implausible or misapplied, the hearer or viewer turns into the outsider and becomes a kind of voyeur watching other people worship. She sits it all out, not caring. It is then time to be fallow before the gifts come again and the table is reset, the song resung.

Anomie, anomy, the second of the obsolete words for a human response, or nonresponse, has come back because it is needed. Anomie is "normlessness," an inability to care about standards when one is sated. Emile Durkheim, the French sociologist, helped restore the notion of anomie to currency. He studied suicide as it occurred not among manna-eaters but those who could regularly count on quail. While one would have expected the poor and hungry to take their own lives, it was the prosperous in well-regulated and secure societies who became dulled, jaded, and after restlessness, depressed.

Anomie is at the root of suburban juvenile delinquency, a cause behind mindless vandalism in the better communities. Anomie is an agent of destruction in the marriages of the affluent. It numbs the sated heart, the one too long full of too many riches. "Cheap grace," Dietrich Bonhoeffer called the too-ready gift and the too-easy acceptance. The fallow heart allows for postponement, economy. It demands patience and waiting. Then there can be a return of norms and standards, a readiness for the first sign that the Giver, not the gift, is to be source and goal of the heart's affections.

Acedia, accedie, is the third of the medieval designations for "leanness in the soul," the wasting disease that comes to the fat and full. The word remains rare, even in the vocabulary of the learned, but the reality to which it points is anything but rare. One of the doctors of the church tried to define it as "sadness in the face of spiritual good." The medievals spoke of "the noonday demon," the kind of ennui that haunted one at midday when there were no shadows. The *daemon meridianus,* the evil spirit of the meridian, inspired one of the capital or deadly sins, which meant it was at the head of a whole column of others.

Unfortunately, it was often translated as "sloth," which today means being lazy, lingering in the tepid bath or the inviting bed. In medieval times, people knew a "sloth" that was more spiritually deadening. Too much leeks and garlic, too many quail—these could lead to boredom as much as manna would. The summery sort of spirituality, in the eyes of those denied the easy access to goods, looks like a kind of abundance for which the wintry sort cannot get "up." First must come a movement of the earth beyond noontime and the sun which creates no darkness. First there must be shadow.

The psalms regularly beckon the pilgrim to a world in which shadows threaten. The shadow, in biblical contexts, implies a drama of contrasts. In the sun is safety, but one does not welcome the promise of safety when there is no need for trust. Trust comes when the enemy lurks in ravines and crevasses of a valley that is nothing but shadow because it is a valley of death. One of the best known lines of all the psalms speaks to this: "Even though I walk through a valley dark as death I fear no evil, for thou art with me, thy staff and thy crook are my comfort" (23:4).

THE VALLEY OF THE SHADOW

A millennium from now believers are likely still to prefer the cadences of the King James Version for that line, "Yea, though I walk through the valley of the shadow of death, I will fear no evil . . ." Death symbolizes all the evils of ravined life, all the perils of the earthly journey. In the psalm that speaks of guidance through the valley, the one who prays is compared to a sheep. Modern urbanites are supposed to have rejected this likeness long ago. The world of pasture and lambs is alien to city experience. It belongs to primitive rural recall. Yet highly sophisticated sufferers who must turn to the wall in the hospital and come to terms with their destiny are as likely to request this psalm from the lips of those who read to the dying as any other text. In the drama of contrast between life and death, the shadows are all gone. The victim is ready to be likened to dumb animals who trust the staff and crook because they have no choice except to trust the one who holds the tools.

When there is still health and vigor, people can show bravado in the face of peril. In the times when one can display macho and some good-natured swagger, they can still invert the meaning of the verse. Now and then on the office wall of someone at midlife and in good health, you will chance to see a wall plaque, Gothic-lettered and apparently overlookable as a too-familiar scripture. You read it casually, until its twist hits you. "Yea, though I walk through the valley of the shadow of death, I will fear no evil, for I am the meanest bastard in the valley." No offense. A good time was had by all, the letterer, the hanger of the plaque, and the reader. The structure of the universe is not jarred by such humor. The overly pious, the pious, and the impious have their differing reactions, none of them necessarily memorable. We can all laugh.

The authors of psalms know who is the meanest bastard in the valley: the letterer, the hanger of the plaque, and the

159

reader all vie for the appellation. Meanness came by choice, bastardy by fate, and together they represent human complicity in problems of violence and the world of shadows. Yet the psalmist knew that if mean bastardy was responsible for getting one into the valley, it was no instrument for swashbuckling one's way through it. The psalmic realism went even further. Not being mean or being born legitimate did not exempt one from having to pass through the valley of the shadow of death. Yet there, only there, where all the muscle and swords were too weak for the forces of threat and attack, there is where the birth of trust came to those who waited in patience.

So rich is the image of the valley of the shadow of death that it almost blocks out the metaphors of winter that we have employed to trace the seasons of the heart. The two are in no way contradictory, however, for the wintry world is a shadowed world, marked by death. And winterfallowing as a strategy for spirituality parallels the psalm's idea of trusting the one who with staff and crook guides through the valley. The relation relies on patience and waiting. Unseeded, uncropped, such soil is not pregnant. It is not ready to burst forth with its own vitalities. Its season will come.

The beginning of return comes with the awakening of experience of almost any sort of emotion. After satiety God sent leanness. After summery joy, there was coldness. Apathy, anomie, acedie are words that offend because they seem remote, but they can also sting when the emotions to which they refer become familiar. *Any* emotions? Already we have seen that the emotion of envy or rage against the enemy was some sort of quickening. It was the base for better actions or emotions.

Psalm 73 combines a number of moods and reactions, all of them potential signs at the end of the period of waiting and patience. Few psalms are more psychologically plausible. The writer acknowledges that his "feet had almost slipped, my foothold had all but given way" (73:2), a position with which all but the most secure can identify. What was so jarring? "The boasts of sinners roused my envy when I saw how they prosper. No pain, no suffering is theirs; they are sleek and sound in limb" (73:3–4). They do not suffer the torments of mortal men, says the eye of righteous envy. They are full and fat, but God did not send them leanness: "Their eyes gleam through folds of fat; while vain fancies pass through their minds" (73:7). They can be as slanderous as the children of Israel were when they yearned to go back to slavery. God does not punish them even though they can say, "What does God know? The Most High neither knows nor cares" (73:11). That double charge is the highest blasphemy, but still their folds of fat grow.

I find it hard to picture many people who would not admit to emotions like those of the psalmist. A couple feels it has played by the rules of the game. Claiming neither heroism nor sainthood, they have been waiting and patient for the stirrings of God. Their God knew their need, and they wanted to grow into responsive knowledge. Their Lord cared, and they reacted by caring for others, for the world, for their selves—including their bodies.

Suddenly one of them falls to illness, not a plague of leanness, but still a "wasting disease." The bodily processes turn corrupt, and cells devour each other while the wasting goes on and the shadows in the valley lengthen. Down the block, looking on under folds of fat on their eyelids are overeaters, overdrinkers, oversmokers, careless and heedless people who evidently prosper. The couple reaches out for names to describe their emotions, for descriptions of their reactions. "We were playing by the rules of the game, yet 'they' changed it." "They?" Not the neighbors, the doctors, or the health experts. They? Faceless, normless, errant cells? Determiners of the rules of the universe? God?

By nature neither envious nor raging, the couple suppress emotions, until good counselors tell them to be honest. Rage, rage, they are told, against the dying of the light and the encroachment of the winter night. Be envious and let envy turn to anger against that universe, and against the Lord who seems to lack control. Rail at "those" who paid no attention to your playing by the rules. Scorn those who ever gave you the idea that you were not alone in that universe, that something or someone cared, that a Yes was there awaiting your Yes, a Thou for your I. Envy and rage at least were better every time than apathy and accedie. They restored the fires and the shadows.

Psychological realism, we have said, characterizes this psalm. In another passage it is likely to evoke assenting response. After comparing the way of the victim with the fat-folded lookers-on, the writer is autobiographically rueful. "So it was all in vain that I kept my heart pure and washed my hands in innocence" (73:13). Here is again a hint of the transactional view, a reminiscence of one way of dealing with God. I will be pure and innocent, it says, and you shall keep me, for my having been fruitful. Then, more revealingly, "Yet had I let myself talk on in this fashion, I should have betrayed the family of God" (73:15). Just as the bartering view of life with God lived in the back of the memory, so responsibility began to return in the midst of envy and rage. I, says the psalmist, owe something to the family of God. I have been a member, perhaps a marginal one, of the company of the respondents to God. If I do not listen to the word that calls forth trust, I violate integrity. I have worked through and past envy and anger, and will not "let myself talk on in this fashion." The winterfallow heart is ready for seed and the possibility of crop.

The problem of evil

Readiness does not mean ripeness. The mystery of what another psalm (49:4) called the riddle, remains. "So I set myself to think this out but I found it too hard for me" (73:16). The summery sort of spirituality never comes to this point. "Christ is the Answer," says its banner, no matter what the question. The Answer addresses all, and solves all, according to bumper stickers. There is no reason to question the piety or the integrity of those who believe and have experienced this answer. They wave arms in the air and dance; they speak in tongues and prophesy; and who is to deny them a place in the family of God? Karl Rahner does advise readers not to allow them the only place, however. The psalmist sides with him. There are mysteries too deep for thinking out successfully, too hard for easy response. The couple who feels "they" have changed the rules of the game may not easily transfer "they" to God, and if they do, the puzzlement grows only worse.

If God is all-powerful, which is one good way to think of a reality for which one reserves the highest name, and God —it bears saying twice—*allows* the suffering, is not this even a worse moral claim in the eyes of those who seem "pure and innocent"? Maybe there is a third way: God *participates* in the life of the people and suffers at their side, thus meriting trust. God may be all-powerful and still may "grow" in converse with the people.

Congregating in the sacred courts

The psalmist undertook a strategy that many moderns who would be spiritual deny themselves. Puzzled by whatever made him a victim, finding answers too hard, he wrote, "I went into God's sacred courts; there I saw clearly what their end would be" (73:17). By now one might seek a higher question than "Why do the careless prosper?" A better one might be "Why do the caring suffer?" Yet the contexts for affirmation in these questions need not differ. Many who claim that God does not become a presence today have not relearned the ancient clue: that there may well be sacred zones where the memory of burning bushes might lead to renewed fires. The still small voice was heard in solitude, but it was prompted by the promise of company. Sacred courts offer the heart reasons which reason does not know. At some stage a spiritual discipline moves from text to context, ancient text to modern context of people.

Sacred courts represent the possibility of what Paul Tillich called "revelatory constellations." The elements of the spiritual universe are there lined up in such a way that they can disclose what had been puzzling darkness. By the end of Psalm 73, even slavery to embitterment and to "the pangs of envy" (73:21) gives way to the Yes. "Yet I am always with thee, thou holdest my right hand; thou dost guide me by thy counsel" (73:23–24). Finally, the sacred points to a presence that transcends the "they" who changed the rules of the game, went beyond the Answers and the questions, went deeper than the puzzlements and hard thoughts.

"Whom have I in heaven but thee? And having thee, I desire nothing else on earth" (73:25). At last, the shift is away from the fullness and fatness that distract, after which God must send leanness. At last, the concern for avoidance of eternal flames and reward of eternal goods can be challenged by the water that quenches the first of these and the fire that burns the second of them. God is loved, beyond the end, for God's sake.

Such a basic turn calls forth more strategies than the one that demands advantageous positioning in the sacred courts.

That observation can sound as cheap as a billboard that says, "Go to the church of your choice." Can the wintry sort of spirituality be appealed to in a setting or assembly where drab and dull people mumble their prose? Organized religion, the institutional church—these are code names for that which suppresses spirituality. They hardly exhaust the reality of what was once meant by "the sacred courts." Many a congregation can induce apathy and pull one down to anomie. Their very celebrations evoke "sadness in the face of spiritual good," and thus accedie. We are then back with all the medieval names and threats, even if the return occurs in the middle of modern times.

To be a modern seeker, agree the scholarly observers, is to seek a spirituality in private, away from the company. Meditation by one's self, reading in the quiet chamber, tuning in to some broadcast message, or linking up with one or two like-minded sorts are the pure and innocent forms of search. All others corrupt because they may connect one with hypocrites or may involve one with busy work. Religion is what one does with one's solitariness; this is the witness of Alfred North Whitehead. Religion has to do with the acts and feelings of the individual by himself or herself. William James, the modern reckoner with varieties of religious experience, testified to that. My own mind is my temple: so trumpeted the defiant political moderns like Tom Paine and Thomas Jefferson. They were all prophets against conventional congregating. They observed others and prescribed for themselves. In their judgment against drab compromise of religion in the assembly, they struck notes that some Hebrew prophets would apparently have understood.

As with prophets, so with mystics: they seek union with the All, the One, and for this they may fallow their spirits. They seek the soul's dark night, and welcome the unknowingness of the heavy cloud of mystery. Behind them is the monastery where colleagues chant psalms. Lost in their past are the props of the community. They may be waiting and patient or they may seek the soul and push for results. Their strategies vary, but their innocence and pureness demand that they shrug off sensation, bodily pleasure, and company —most of all, company.

The psalmist, to a point, sounded like the modern individualist or the medieval mystic. In the end he had no one to rely on in heaven or earth except the Lord who reached out a hand to guide. Yet the pureness and innocence of the search led the seeker eventually to the zone where community gathers. The bricks in the chapel wall in our time may very well seem sanctified by the prayers of people who through centuries in their commonness knelt near them. The sweat and odor of the fellow worshipers may compete with his private incense, but embodiment afflicts one creatively with an awareness that the Presence comes in a world where sense and body are honored. One does indeed compromise in the company of others, but there, too, a worshiper draws on a broader language of spirituality. Who but the community has kept alive the word that comes from the canon? Who else translates the systems of language from the page of the text back to or ahead to the living and surprising words of judgment and life?

Someone has said that people who seek the excitement of seeing trains pass should not complain that the trains do not go by the breakfast window if they have moved to a house away from the tracks. The sacred courts are not the only place where the psalmist could move beyond his puzzlement and hard questions. These courts nevertheless did represent one place where the transcendent might impinge.

The soul in a fallow period may move into the company at sacred courts. For some, an organist practicing on a Saturday afternoon in an empty church will evoke memories of childhood churchgoing back when a naive faith welcomed the Presence. Now, a generation having passed, the one who quietly listens to that organ may learn to suspend disbelief and find a possibility that the empty church could be part of the sacred courts. The sound of the pipes and reeds connotes hymns that came from the depths of the very earth which shouts and sings. A tourist becomes a pilgrim through such listening. Not content to be a dilettante or voyeur, she kneels. There, where prayers of common people have been raised for centuries, she becomes a peasant in the courts of the Lord. Or marginal congregation members may suspend the judgment that all around are hypocrites. We may then see them provisionally as puzzled people who are pressing ahead in the face of hard questions. They, too, feel envious and angered over the changed rules of the game. In their seeking they provide the company in which a Yes can first reappear.

The organ, the stones of the wall, and the bent knee—all these connote and evoke longing: "I pine, I faint with longing for the courts of the Lord's temple; my whole being cries out with joy to the living God. Even the sparrow finds a home, and the swallow has her nest, where she rears her brood beside thy altars" (84:2–3). That psalm sees as "happy the men whose refuge is in thee, whose hearts are set on the pilgrim ways" (84:5). *Pilgrim* ways: there is no stopping in this refuge, and there never was. Pilgrims "pass on from outer wall to inner, and the God of gods shows himself in Zion" (84:7). These need not be the walls of literal courts, altars, and sanctuaries; even the psalmist immediately moved to metaphor. Pilgrims pass through thirsty valleys seeking springs, toward pools to quench thirst. When thirsty, one goes to the well, not to the altar (84:6). What matters is the longing that leans toward a realization that

"Better one day in thy courts than a thousand days at home; better to linger by the threshold of God's house than to live in the dwellings of the wicked" (84:10).

THE PASSAGE BETWEEN SEASONS

The threshold, the *limen,* is located at the transit between worlds. Victor Turner has given to the spiritual vocabulary an understanding of the liminal experiences. The initiate is a person on pilgrimage who converts from one way or stage to another. He moves toward and across a threshold, toward a new resolution. The threshold is neither here nor there. As a liminal place, it allows for support of neither the props of the old way or the community of a new company. For the moment, the person in motion is in a sense of suspension and even feels abandonment. In our image, this is winterfallow time, a time of readiness for seeding and crop.

"When foundations are undermined, what can the good man do?" (11:3). The wintry sort of spirituality moves on a landscape where drift of snow and shift of footing are taken for granted as they would be literally in snow on a glacier. Are there no fixed points? The next verse hurries with, "The Lord is in his holy temple" (11:4), "his face is turned towards the upright man" (11:7).

The Lord in the temple evokes an image of space. God, the high God, remains above all. In the psalmist's world the dark universe promotes the sense of human smallness and does so toward creative ends. "When I look up at thy heavens, the work of thy fingers, the moon and the stars set in their place by thee, what is man that thou shouldst remember him, mortal man that thou shouldst care for him?" (8:3–4). A very modern-minded theologian in the early years of satellites and space objects reports that he took his eleven year old into the yard under the night sky. "Which ones did we put up there?" asked the young Promethean. The story by now is dated. The technological mastery implied in the boy's question is no longer an idol. The "we," the nation that did the lofting, is less sure of its purposes now. A generation has passed. The odds are good that the boy, toward middle years, is in a backyard with *his* child. He and she again become aware of the need for wonder on a winter night.

They are small, benign, these "thinking reeds." They feel smaller as their wonder grows. But by acts of empathy they may again be closer to the psalmist than to the space-shooter. "What is man that thou shouldst remember him, mortal man that thou shouldst care for him?" (8:4). We are back to Genesis 1 and the chaos at whose edge humans live. Wonder brings surprise: now when the human is smallest and life seems most brief, the world in front of the text offers new possibilities. The grandeur remains. "Yet thou hast made him little less than a god, crowning him with glory and honour" (8:5). As often in the psalms, the Yes breaks in precisely when one is ready for the No. When the psalmist and the backyard child are being taught reduction, their being expands. They respond as singular creatures.

THE VALUES OF HOPE AND FIDELITY

Singularly, people full of wonder also hope. Adam and Eve could not have both immortality and knowledge. They chose knowledge of their creaturehood and introduced the burdens that went with it. With those burdens came hope, an evident element in the human makeup. So strong is hope, said Viktor Frankl, that some held to it even in the death camps. It is so potent, we say, that "nothing shall separate" the hoper from God in Christ, nothing including principalities and powers and death. That hope impresses not when folds of fat fall over eyes or when paths drip fatness or when God sends quail two cubits deep. It comes after the heart attack or while cells waste and friends withdraw because they are unable to bear the sight of the horror. Then it is that nothing separates the creature from God.

"Thou art my hope, O Lord, my trust, O Lord, since boyhood" (71:5). The summery sort can say more easily, "Thou art my having, my fulfillment." The wintry sort, there on the terrain in solidarity with those who exclude God from their horizon, must wager. The text bids for a suspension of disbelief in hope. Try this, it says, as another mode of being a possibility for you. The psalmist knows that God is able to "stand aloof from me" (71:12). Therefore prayer is necessary. Chosen answers are not guaranteed. "I will wait in continual hope" (71:14). In unnecessary modesty, the psalmist provides poetic lines for the children of centuries to come: "Thou shalt ever be the theme of my praise, although I have not the skill of a poet" (71:15).

Hope on the winterfallow landscape tells a story that is remembered and hoped for at once: "Thou hast made me pass through bitter and deep distress, yet dost revive me once again and lift me again from earth's watery depths" (71:20). Therefore, "I will sing thee psalms" (71:23).

Summery and wintry sorts of spirituality are not chemically pure, said Karl Rahner, and we should not be rigid in separating them. In the hope beyond hope they at least meet: "He brought me out into an open place, he rescued me because he delighted in me" (18:19). These lines close a psalm that well depicted the hemmed-in character of existence. "In anguish of heart I cried to the Lord" (18:6). Anguish, *angustiae,* angst, anxiety: the words blur into each other. Together they tell of life in the "narrows." There are the snares, the destructive torrents (18:4,5). There, in the narrows, "he reached down from the height and took me" (18:16). The "open place" comes from the context of Hebrew words that translate to those we use today for "being saved."

The summery sort asks, "Are you saved?" and before considering what being saved means, or from what or for what or through what instrument ("Jesus Saves!") saving comes, he continues, "I am saved!" The wintry sort does not disdain this experience, though she may be put off by the braggadocio of some or the belligerence of others of the saved. She is likely to foresee the large place still partly in the language of hope and wager. "Deliverance is near to those who worship him" (85:9). And a surprising bond develops: "Love and fidelity have come together; justice and peace join hands. Fidelity springs up from earth" (85:10–11).

Fidelity, *creative* fidelity, Gabriel Marcel called it. There is tension between creativity and fidelity. *Mere* fidelity can be static, lifeless. *Mere* creativity is likely to be restless and self-arrogating. Taken together, they represent human possibility in the face of divine repose. The winterfallow land is seeded when fidelity is creative; it has gone to seed when it is merely fidelity. Deliverance is always near, always in the process of coming toward fulfillment: that is the message of these wintry psalms when they beckon for a Yes.

The wintry sort, in the end, does seek a security that is attached through fidelity to the secure source, the Presence, the Thou. "The Lord is close to those whose courage is broken and he saves those whose spirit is crushed" (34:18). In the end, despite the psalms' riddles and hard questions trust can grow along with hope. There on the horizon next to the horizon of those who have seen God excluded, remain people in whom the mystery of faith grows. They call the seeding "grace" and the crops, "gifts."

The disciplines of spirituality allow for both mystical ascent to God and prophetic stabs at the divine heart. Different winterers will have varying paces of change till they come to awareness of their Yes. Some will be surprised on the snowscape in the midst of the dark of winter night, when moments of astonishing clarity offer promise. Others must scan the horizon and be content with small signs no richer than the glow of a candle in a distant cabin of refuge. Yet a wintry sort of spirituality also produces occasions when the Absence leaves the horizon and the Presence realizes itself. "The Lord is close to those whose courage is broken and he saves those whose spirit is crushed" (34:18).

The Presence then comes so close that you can sense it. On the wintry landscape, the searcher hears psalms sung, sees pilgrim bands, smells the incense of restored prayer, touches the company of the faithful, and even tastes. Father Divine, a black "deity," liked to say that he "tangibilificated" God. One might speak of this Presence on the horizon as being touchable in its impending nearness: here is what we may call the "palpabilification" of God. The psalmist had a word for that, too, a promise after the fallow season: "Taste, then, and see that the Lord is good" (34:8). "For those who fear him lack nothing" (34:9). "Those who seek the Lord lack no good thing" (34:10). One hopes.